THE RISE OF CAMELOT

THE RISE OF CAMELOT

A Modern-Day True Tale of Horses, Dragons, and a Girl with a Dream

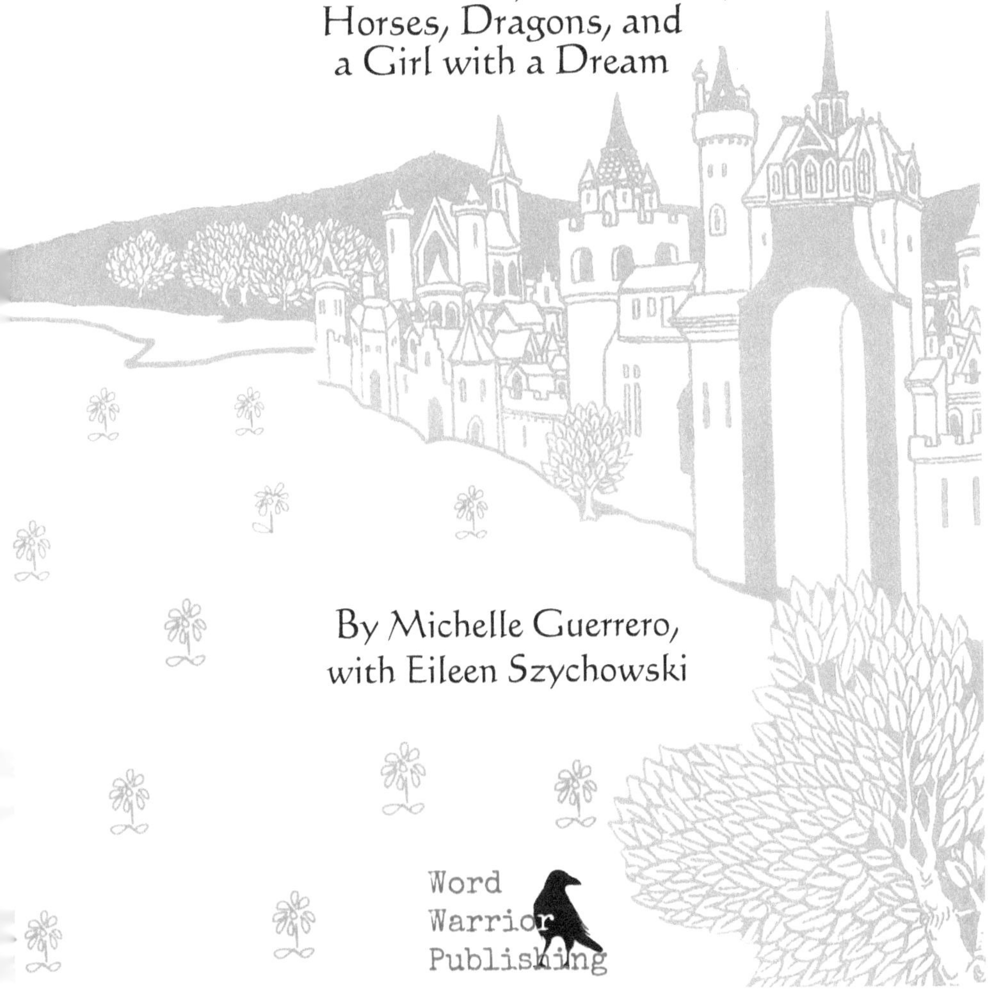

By Michelle Guerrero,
with Eileen Szychowski

Word
Warrior
Publishing

Word Warrior Publishing
info@wordwarriorpublishing.com

First Edition: August 2023

This book is a biography, and it reflects Eileen Szychowski's recollections. Only the names of a few minors have been changed and some dialogue has been recreated. The author has made every attempt to tell the story with accuracy.

The Rise of Camelot, A Modern-Day True Tale of Horses, Dragons, and A Girl with a Dream: a biography by Michelle Guerrero with Eileen Szychowski - 1st ed.

Edited by Casie Bazay

Cover art adapted from Arthur Pyle's *The Lady of ye Lake* (1903) and Aubrey Beardsley, from *Le Morte Darthur* (1893-94). Both Pyle and Beardsley's work appear in Camelot Chronicles, the newsletter produced by Camelot Therapeutic Horsemanship. *The Lady of ye Lake* illustration was at the top of Eileen Szychowski's articles titled: Be It Known That… The Lady of the Lake presented Arthur with Excalibur. Many of the ink images throughout were adapted from artwork by Aubrey Beardsley.

Printed in the United States of America

979-8-9871321-2-8 (hardcover)
979-8-9871321-3-5 (paperback)
979-8-9871321-4-2 (ebook)

No matter who you are, where you come from, or what you look like, you are God's gift to the world. Believe in yourself! – E.S.

For the dreamers whose hearts thump to the sound of hooves. – M.G.

CONTENTS

The Queendom

FOREWORD

Mark Bogosian
Director, Quality of Life Grants Program
Christopher & Dana Reeve Foundation

The late actor, film star, director, and activist Christopher Reeve once said, "A hero is an ordinary individual who finds the strength to persevere and endure in spite of overwhelming obstacles." Christopher knew a lot about heroes. Many people knew him for playing Superman in the movies and for his work as a disability activist after he became paralyzed. You, my fellow reader and adventurer, are about to embark on a magical journey to the real-life Camelot. A journey of peaks and valleys, overcoming obstacles, and dragon slaying; and on this journey, you will meet an incredible, real-life hero, Eileen Szychowski.

Eileen is a trailblazer! She possesses a strength forged in fire—much like Merlin's sword, Excalibur. She teaches us all the important lessons, through her actions and accomplishments, to turn obstacles into opportunities. But I won't tell you her story here, as that would ruin the great experience you are about to have as you turn the pages, as I did, discovering all about this amazing role model.

There are many incredible, beautiful lessons you will learn as you read about this remarkable pioneer and her groundbreaking achievements. Many of these lessons she received from her own personal Merlin. Much like the mystical mentor who imparted his wisdom and guidance to King Arthur, Eileen's real-life, yet equally magical mentor Josef Rivers had perhaps the greatest impact on Eileen. He bestowed upon her the lessons that permeate this story. Lessons about rising to your highest good. Lessons about equality and learning from each other. Lessons about using our differences to work together and create a better world for everyone. But the one that struck me most—the one I hope you will embrace and keep close to your heart—is that success can only be kept when it is given away. If you don't understand what that means yet, you will when you've reached the end of this book. Eileen's tale is a success story on so many levels, mostly because of how freely she gave and continues to give to this day.

Near the end, you will read about the real-life Camelot, Camelot Therapeutic Horsemanship in Scottsdale, Arizona. A place "where heroes are born" and where children and adults with disabilities can experience the magic of horses. You'll later read that, "Everyone who came to Camelot realized they were part of something special." That's how I feel being a part of the Christopher & Dana Reeve Foundation where we are dedicated to curing spinal cord injury by advancing innovative research and improving quality of life for individuals and families impacted by paralysis. Through the Foundation, we run the National Paralysis Resource Center, which offers a constellation of free services, programs, and informational support for people living with paralysis and their caregivers. I am so privileged and honored to be a part of that work, and I know that's how everyone at Camelot feels as well.

Our founder, Christopher Reeve, also said, "So many of our dreams at first seem impossible, then they seem improbable, and then, when we summon the will, they soon become inevitable." That quote mirrors the life so passionately lived by Eileen. Her example, along with this book, charges all of us to summon the will to live a life in which we pursue and live our dreams and to give them away, thereby creating success for everyone with whom we share them.

In the spirit of this book, may we each live our lives with courage and determination to pursue our dreams, and may we slay some dragons along the way! Now, saddle up and onward to Camelot!

PREFACE

Camelot is a real place that sits in the heart of the Sonoran Desert of Arizona. There's a powerful energy felt by most who enter her gates. Some people attribute it to the serene setting or the animals. Some can't quite put their finger on it but know they're someplace sacred.

There's magic deep in the soul of Camelot that grew from a profound love of horses and people. It flourished from a desire to make horse dreams come true. Good intentions as strong as these radiate; they float on the breeze, hum through the horses, and land in the hearts of everyone in the queendom.

There are uncanny parallels between the girl who raised Camelot in the desert and the boy who raised England's Camelot during medieval times. They both fought for justice. They lived their lives with chivalry. And they each had a mystical mentor who always seemed to be at least two steps ahead of everyone else. He helped them realize their potential and guided them to their destiny.

This is the story about the girl who built Camelot.

The Redwood Forest

"It simply isn't an adventure worth telling if there aren't any dragons."
J.R.R.Tolkien

CHAPTER 1

It's written that Merlin lived time backwards, which made him the best kind of tutor for the Wart, an ordinary young man who grew into a king and ruled Camelot. While some argue the facts surrounding Merlin and the legend of King Arthur and his kingdom, I can assure you the stories of Eileen Szychowski ("sha-husky") and her Camelot are true. A believer might say that history repeated itself centuries later when Merlin was born to tutor an ordinary girl who would raise Camelot once again.

For those of you who aren't sure if you believe in the mystical, you might find yourself a believer in the end. Or is it the beginning? In the spirit of Merlin, this story begins somewhere in the middle, tucked in the Santa Cruz Mountains in California where Eileen lived on 150 acres of farmland that was owned by her Italian grandparents. A magical land abundant with orchards, vineyards, and ancient redwood trees with arms that touched the sky.

Eileen wrestled with a stray thought as she galloped through a field in her imagination on the back of a beautiful horse. It didn't matter what the horse looked like because when you love them, they're all magnificent. She could almost feel the wind rush through her long, dark hair.

The sound of tires crunching on the pavement outside her grandparents' country store helped her win the wrestling match with her daydream. She shoved it in a box and slammed the lid. Dreams like that could only end in heartache for someone like her. She believed with certainty that after high school she'd go to college and end up with a desk job. As the daughter of a military man, she was practical, even at sixteen.

Eileen narrowed her green eyes, which were sometimes blue depending on the day, at the man who walked through the door. She knew most of the people who shopped at the country store in the heart of their tight-knit, rural community. Farmers, ranchers, and working-class families came in for all their essentials. And since the internet as we know it wasn't invented in 1969, they also came in for the latest bits of gossip or to search ads on the bulletin board. Working behind the counter in the summer was a decent trade-off for an allowance.

Eileen was curious about the unusual-looking man who got out of the truck. He was handsome like an **aristocrat**, but older like her dad. He walked to the door with an extremely difficult gait; it was much more than a limp. But what really got her attention was the small animal tucked in the crook of his arm. He made his way into the store and placed the animal on the counter in front of her.

"Would you mind keeping an eye on it for a moment?" he asked with a smooth English accent.

Would I mind? "I'd love to do, but what is this little thing?" she asked.

"It's a baby African Pygmy goat. I raise them along with other animals at my ranch up the road."

He selected a cold soda and asked Eileen about herself. She was fascinated by him and completely forgot that he, like her, was noticeably disabled.

"Do you like horses?" he asked.

"I'm crazy about horses and always have been."

And that's when the first invitation from the Universe arrived.

The man, who introduced himself as Josef Rivers, told Eileen that he ran a horse ranch up on Laurel Glen Road and gave riding lessons to kids with disabilities, all at no charge.

Why would this man, who knows nothing about me, be interested in offering me free horseback riding lessons unless there was something in it for himself? Was he one of those creepy old men who preyed on young girls, the kind my mother had warned me about?

"Thank you," she said. "I'll think about it."

But she did no such thing. The offer was too good to be true, so she shoved the thought in the box where horse dreams lived and clicked the lid shut. The mysterious man walked out the door and she never saw him in the shop again.

Eileen and Arthur's tale began centuries apart in England. The once and future Queen of Camelot was born of ordinary means in Cambridgeshire on July 29, 1953. For most of her growing-up years, she moved from country to country with her parents, two younger brothers, and older sister because her father was in the U.S. Air Force.

From the time she was able to blow out birthday candles, she wished for the same thing year after year: a horse—not a pony, mind you, but a horse. Since her family moved often to different countries, they couldn't have pets. But to her advantage, Europe was full of horses.

In England, she lived near London and was captivated by the tall black beauties of The Queen's Life Guard. They were ridden by troopers of the Mounted Regiment, dressed in their ceremonial red tunics and thigh-high black boots that gleamed in the sunlight.

When her father was transferred to Turkey, she would chase after carriage horses as they passed on their way to the bazaar in hopes to pet a nose. The drivers were always kind and allowed her to love on them. She had a Turkish neighbor who would let her ride bareback on their farm horses.

In Germany, there were the large Percheron and Belgian draft horses that pulled beer wagons at Oktoberfest celebrations.

On a summer road trip through the Austrian Alps with her family, her nose was pressed up against the window every time they encountered a Haflinger pulling a wagon loaded with freshly cut hay. Their large eyes and golden manes and tails were the stuff of fairytales.

Her desire for a horse sat deep in her soul. But the stars said, "Not yet."

In 1964, Eileen was ten and a half years old and attending school on the base where her father was stationed in Germany when she got sick. She had a rare neuro-muscular disease called Guillain-Barre Syndrome. Later it became the chronic progressive form and is what caused her disability. Her family moved back to the United States so that she could get the best medical care at Walter Reed Army Hospital, not far from Fort Meade, Maryland, where her father would be stationed for the next three and a half years.

She learned a great many things during this time while learning to live life differently. One of the most critical lessons was patience. The other was perseverance.

CHAPTER 2

Eileen looked down at her hands, now paralyzed. *They make everything harder.* A year and a half ago she didn't have to think twice about things like dressing, fastening buttons, combing her hair, and pretty much everything else associated with getting ready in the morning. Now, with the paralysis in her hands and wrists, everything required more thought and a lot of extra time. Fortunately, the strength in her upper arms had nearly returned to normal, thanks to many long months of rehabilitation and physical therapy at Walter Reed Hospital. This enabled her to accomplish these tasks in unusual ways.

Being a middle schooler was difficult. Having a disability was even more problematic. But what really poked at her heart was knowing that she looked different from everyone else. Her body hadn't begun to grow curves like the other girls, and she never quite knew if eyes turned her way because she was the new kid or if it was because she walked differently.

There's no blending into the middle school crowd when walking down the hall using crutches. Her metal leg braces that stretched all the way up to her hips were difficult to hide too, but necessary if she wanted to walk. She was always grateful to make it to her desk chair without incident. Falls happened more than she cared to admit. Eileen always tried to get a spot closest to the window so she could see what was going on outside. She sighed quietly in relief from the safety of her chair and searched the field for the hawk she often saw there.

She glanced around the classroom, and like always, she was the only student there who looked like her. Most kids who had disabilities in the 1960s weren't educated in regular public schools but rather in special schools that kept them apart from other kids their age.

A twinge of discomfort flared in the pit of Eileen's stomach as Jana made her way down the aisle. She was passing out small pink envelopes—invitations, no doubt. The blonde with a ponytail twisted a ringlet around her finger and whispered something about a birthday party. She was three desks away when a door slammed making Eileen jump.

"Everyone to their seats, please," said the teacher. She glared over the rim of her glasses that sat low on her nose. "You can pass those out after class. This isn't social time."

"Yes ma'am," said Jana and she scurried to her seat.

The tension in Eileen's chest relaxed and she let out a little sigh of relief. Not being able to be invited was loads better than not actually being asked. She couldn't remember the last time someone wanted her to come to a party or a sleepover. She was even passed up for most school activities. But still, she had to wonder if perhaps there was an invitation with her name on it in Jana's pile of envelopes. She bit her lip and looked down at her desk.

Jana would have walked right past me like I wasn't even here. But at least invisible is better than being in the spotlight.

Eileen did her best to pay attention to the history lesson, but her thoughts wandered down another path. Most people who survive the acute period of Guillain-Barré Syndrome eventually regain all lost functions. Her doctors thought she would too. Eileen wondered when that day would come.

Something outside the window caught her eye.

The hawk.

She nearly said it aloud because he surprised her. The powerful bird hovered over the field before swiftly diving into the grasses below. She sat up taller to try and see if he had caught something, but he was lost in the tall grasses. As if to answer her question, he hopped into a nearby tree with something furry grasped in the claws of one of his feet while he balanced precariously on the other.

Eileen smiled and cocked her head, looking at the hawk, who seemed to look right back at her.

Nice catch!

She couldn't help but feel a connection with the bird who frequently showed up for her during class. She didn't know what it meant, but her feathered friend brought her joy.

CHAPTER 3

In 1968, Eileen's father was transferred to an air base on the island of Hokkaido in northern Japan. Since there were no American middle schools or high schools on the island, her parents decided it would be best if her father went to this deployment alone while the rest of the family moved to Santa Cruz, where her mom's family lived. This way, her mom would have support from relatives, and Eileen and her siblings could all graduate from the same local high school. Eileen was familiar with Santa Cruz, having spent a few months there with her Italian grandparents while her dad studied Russian at the Defense Language Institute Foreign Language Center nearby in Monterey. But this would be the first time she called the town home.

High school looked a lot like middle school. Once again, she was the new kid, but one thing had changed for the better. She had recovered some strength in her hips, enabling her to trade in the hip-high leg braces for knee-high leg braces. These shorter ones allowed her to bend her knees as she walked, and, better yet, they could be worn under her slacks. Another improvement in high school was that there wasn't a dress code. Wearing jeans over the shorter braces made her feel as if she didn't stick out quite as much as before.

Getting a driver's license is considered a rite of passage for American teens. The fact that there was no public transportation in the Santa Cruz Mountains fueled her desire to drive into a white-hot flame. She knew driving was her path to independence and to making friends. And while she was grateful for the job at her grandmother's store, she wanted something different for her future and she needed a way to get there.

At sixteen she was more than ready and took driver's education with the rest of her junior class, but it was strictly a classroom subject with no behind-the-wheel training. Driver's training was available to all who passed driver's ed. But unlike her peers, she couldn't sign up for that class because there wasn't an adaptive driving program available for high school students who had disabilities.

She would be forced to wait until she was eighteen, then she'd be eligible for Vocational Rehabilitation Services. This agency funded adaptive driver training for people with disabilities who were in college or another employment training program. There was also one other obstacle in her path: her loved ones.

"I have no social life," Eileen said. "The only interaction I have with peers is when I'm working the store!" She was convinced that driving would change all of this.

But some of her family worried it would be dangerous, if not impossible, for her to even attempt to learn to drive. They had never seen people driving with hand controls and couldn't imagine it.

"It's too dangerous," they said. "There's no way you'll be able to react in time."

"It's not dangerous with hand controls," she countered. "I've seen how they work, and I can do this."

Once, a polio survivor drove up to the country store using hand controls, and the customer was happy to show Eileen how they worked. They could even be adapted for a driver who lacked grip strength. While the lever that operated the gas pedal and brakes would not be a problem for her, controlling the steering wheel would be a different story. But there was a solution to this too. A small cradle-like device that swiveled could be fitted onto the steering wheel. Placing the right hand snugly into the cradle would enable the driver to securely turn the steering wheel in both directions.

She was confused by her parents' refusal to sign the permission form. They never stood in the way of her doing things that made her more independent.

If only they could understand how hand controls worked.

Once she turned eighteen, parental permission wasn't required. Jane Farmer, her Vocational Rehabilitation counselor, arranged for Eileen to receive adaptive driver training. It wasn't until her driver training instructor, Sam, came into her life that her family started to come around. Sam, who was a certified adaptive driving instructor, had seen other families struggle like this before and was able to provide them with information and support to help them overcome their fear and resistance.

"People with disabilities need to be able to drive just as much as anyone else if they are to experience success in life," he said. "And they actually have better driving records than drivers without disabilities."

He helped ease their doubts and Eileen started her driver training with him at eighteen. Sam was encouraging and supportive. She aced the driving test and immediately got her license. Getting a car would take a little longer though.

Eileen was patient and determined. She saved for two years and when she was twenty, she purchased her first, used car. There was nothing fancy or cool about the large, dark red Ford sedan, but it didn't matter to her one bit. It represented freedom and that was the only thing that mattered. The Department of Vocational Rehabilitation paid for the installation of the hand controls that she needed to drive her new wheels.

Two weeks after she purchased the car, Eileen moved out of her parents' house. A young woman she knew from high school was looking for a roommate to share her apartment in town. Eileen was happy to rent the room. Living independently made going to Cabrillo College easier now that she could drive herself to school. And she was right about the friends too. It wasn't just because she owned a car, it was about independence and accessibility. Her wheels could get her where she needed to go, which made a social life possible. She was free.

After sharing an apartment for about a year and a half, Eileen was ready to try living solo. She found an affordable one-bedroom apartment not far from the community college and took the next step in independent living. While some things like grocery shopping and laundry would definitely be more challenging, it was a risk worth taking for the complete freedom it would offer.

When Eileen set her mind to something, she did it. She wanted her driver's license; she made it happen. She knew she would go to college, and she did that too. She also knew she would get a desk job instead of something outdoors or with horses like her heart craved. She was right, at least at first.

CHAPTER 4

Eileen's second invitation from the Universe arrived in the 1970s. She was going to school at the University of California, Santa Cruz. Eileen figured she'd become a counselor or social worker because both required language skills instead of manual **dexterity**. College was physically demanding. Getting from class to class with supplies and books is difficult while walking with crutches.

School also took a mental toll. Being different carries an enormous stigma, and it's a heavy burden to carry. Even years away from middle school, she was still the only one in the room like her. She was loads more confident than her thirteen-year-old self but couldn't shake that familiar self-consciousness that accompanied her differences.

The other thing that hadn't changed was her grand passion for horses. The lid on the box of her horse dreams and musings was still closed—most days. She kept it safe next to her heart and only let them out to play on occasion. She didn't really have a choice in the matter. Some dreams are too powerful to contain. Even she wasn't that strong.

Occasionally, one of them led her to a local riding stable. Her smile widened and her spirit soared at even the sight of a horse. She ran her hand along the neck of a curious bay that came over to the fence. She took a deep breath committing the horse's scent to memory.

I won't wash my hands for a week, my new friend.

But then inevitably, she was reminded why she did her best to keep that lid snapped tight. So many, "can'ts and couldn'ts" came next.

The instructors couldn't imagine how they could get someone like her on a horse.

They couldn't envision how someone with her hands could control one.

There was too much liability for them to even try.

Eventually, even with her powerful, renegade dreams, she stopped believing it would happen. Eileen felt defeated and even tried to put a lock on the box.

Message received. I'll always love horses, but I can't realistically see how I can have any real involvement with them.

Unbeknownst to her, her dreams were entangled with her destiny. There was one person in the world who knew. A man Eileen hadn't given a second thought about in years. One who already had plans to help her free those dreams for good.

Eileen's Uncle Bill was a lifelong member of the Elks, a service club that did charity work in the community. During one of their meetings, a man with an English accent came to speak to the group. His name was Josef Rivers. He had purchased a large piece of property in the nearby town of Aptos to expand his therapeutic riding program. Bill was a heavy equipment operator by trade and a good man by heart. He volunteered his services and equipment to cut the program's new riding arena.

Even though Josef hadn't seen Eileen since that day he set a baby goat on the counter in front of her, he somehow knew that Bill was her uncle. Invitation number two came in the form of a pamphlet from Rivers Crest Dragon Slayers. Josef gave it to Bill that day to give to his niece.

When Eileen read the pamphlet, what stood out most wasn't that he might be able to give her riding lessons or that services were offered at no charge, it was the use of the word, "handicapped". Rivers Crest Dragon Slayers was a place where "handicapped" kids and adults could ride.

Handicapped. This word was used a lot before the **Americans with Disabilities Act**. It stemmed from the words "cap in hand", a centuries-old phrase that meant someone who begged for a living. In the 1800s, it evolved as a common way to describe people who had disabilities.

She remembered the fascinating man she met all those years ago, who also had a disability, but the word "handicapped" stopped her in her tracks. At the time, the word handicapped meant "less than" to a lot of people, including Eileen. She never fully recovered like doctors thought she would. She was **quadraparetic**, different from **quadriplegic**. She had partial paralysis in four parts of her body (both arms and legs), but she was more than the word "handicapped".

She scrunched her nose like the word "handicapped" made the pamphlet smell bad. She just couldn't.

Invitation number two got thrown out with the trash. There is great power in words and if she was brutally honest with herself, she was embarrassed to be included in a group called handicapped, which makes what happened next even more miraculous.

"Like everyone else, I, too, saw people with disabilities as 'less than'. In fact, one of the other reasons I resisted exploring Josef's ranch was my embarrassment at being around other people with disabilities. I didn't want the world to think that I was like them. In fact, the last thing I could ever imagine myself doing was working with people with disabilities. It seems the Universe/God/destiny had other plans for me and refused to give up on me, even when I was limiting myself," said Eileen decades later.

CHAPTER 5

Invitation number three arrived when Eileen was 22 years old, seven years after she first met the man in the country store and a few since she tossed his pamphlet into the trash. It was 1976, the year of the bicentennial, America's 200th birthday. The Americans With Disabilities Act (ADA) was not yet in existence, so, as most Americans were celebrating 200 years of freedom, people with disabilities continued to encounter **discrimination** and exclusion in every area of life: at school, in the workplace, on the playground, and in society in general.

Eileen was nearly finished with her bachelor's degree in psychology when she decided to take a break from school. She was exhausted from dealing with the never-ending obstacles of navigating a hilly campus and living independently in an apartment in town. Taking a year off would allow her to recharge her batteries and hopefully get some work experience.

The only job she'd ever had was in her family's country store. It was hardly enough to give her a sense of what her capabilities were, let alone land a job in the field of social services. She turned to her vocational rehabilitation counselor, Jane Farmer. Eileen always felt supported by Jane, who now arranged for Eileen to have two, six-month paid internships as a classroom aide.

The first internship was at the juvenile detention center, where she would meet and become great friends with Mark Mathews, who taught in the classroom at the locked facility.

The second internship was at a school for children with special needs. This was prior to the enactment of laws requiring children with disabilities be educated in a regular classroom with their non-disabled peers.

Eileen was grateful for the opportunity. It helped her zero in on the area in which she hoped to find employment. Working at the detention center with at-risk youth was fulfilling, and she could see herself working in the field. Since each internship was a part-time position, she had some time off during the week to get some rest and do other things.

Even though she had resigned her fate to an indoor desk job, her heart screamed to work with youth or outdoors doing something with nature. But there were no jobs like that for someone like her in the 1970s. She felt stuck in a hole she couldn't figure out how to climb out of with crutches.

But she had this reoccurring dream that sometimes made her wonder. In the dream she was standing on the top of a hill, looking out at the wide valley below. She lifted her arms and crutches, moving them up and down until they morphed into wings. And then she soared like a bird, soaking in the scenery below. There was something more for her out there. She could feel it.

One day she came across an advertisement in the paper for the Budweiser Clydesdale team and hitch. They were coming to the Santa Cruz County Fairgrounds for an exhibition. She wasn't going to miss seeing those beautiful giants up close.

There's a theory among horse lovers that their passion runs as deep as their DNA. Eileen's horse gene was passed to her from her Italian grandmother. Eileen invited her eighty-year-old nonna to come see the Clydesdales.

The parking area was a long walk from the exhibition area and Eileen couldn't find handicapped parking. As she and her grandmother walked to the barn, she kept her eyes open for anyone in a wheelchair who might know where it was for next time.

They made it to the stable and Eileen saw a man sitting in a wheelchair, surrounded by a group of young people and some children with disabilities.

"I wonder where they parked?" she said to her grandmother.

The closer they got the more familiar he looked. It was Josef Rivers, along with some of his volunteers and students. In his eyes was recognition and on his lips was a warm, knowing smile, ready and eager to deliver invitation number three.

"Well, hello there. How have you been?" he asked. The warmth and gracious quality of his voice was inviting.

"I've been doing well, thank you," said Eileen.

"What have you been up to since I saw you last?"

"I've been going to school and working part-time."

"Why don't you and your grandmother sit with our group, and we can catch each other up?"

They accepted his cordial invitation and took a seat in the stable viewing area next to Josef. He filled her in on the newly completed riding facility in the redwood forest on the outskirts of Aptos, a small seaside community not far from Cabrillo College. The new facility offered his students a larger and much more **accessible** environment in which to ride and work with horses.

"Do come and see me up there. I think you'll be pleasantly surprised." He invited her once again, this time with an unmistakable twinkle in his eye.

Okay, she thought to herself as she drove her grandmother home. *This is the third time this man's path has crossed mine, and he's invited me to come visit his ranch. I don't think this is a coincidence. I think it's time for me to go and check it out.*

Invitation number three from the Universe to Eileen Szychowski would not be denied. She was certain she was going to find a pony-ride-operation with disabled people being led around on aged, decrepit horses. But she'd at least check it out since the Universe was so persistent. She waited until the following Monday to call the number on the brochure that Josef gave her, *again.* An appointment for a tour was set for the end of the week.

The day arrived to meet with Josef at the stables. She dressed in jeans and a long-sleeved pullover sweater just in case it was foggy and cool in Aptos. The town lay between the beach and a well-known state park, the Forest of Nicene Marks. Within the park, there were a few privately owned properties, including Rivers Crest Stables, home of the Dragon Slayers.

The drive to Aptos was about twenty minutes from her apartment. Once she reached the edge of town, she took the turn-off into the state park. Immediately the temperature dropped, and she became surrounded by ancient redwoods. She rolled down the window to take in the scent of the trees and the chatter of blue jays. They hopped from tree to tree, scolding the other birds for venturing into their territory. The sunlight streamed through breaks in the canopy highlighting the ferns and forget-me-nots growing along the banks of the dirt road that wound its way through the great trees. She crossed Aptos Creek two or three times before reaching her destination. Following Josef's precise directions, she crossed over the metal bridge high above the creek and turned left onto the curving driveway that would bring her to the stable.

Eileen's jaw dropped when she encountered the reality of River's Crest Stables.

CHAPTER 6

Eileen's breath caught in her chest as she took in the magnificent horses and the exotic creatures ambling about River's Crest Stables. The place seemed to be guarded by the great redwood tree forest that surrounded them.

A tall man riding an elegant bay horse trotted in the outdoor arena. He wore a big smile on his face and Eileen couldn't help but wish it was her riding the horse. She later found out his name was Mike and that he was a schoolteacher. He was also **blind**.

Josef walked toward her, and she was reminded he had a substantial disability involving his legs. But this awareness dissipated like a breeze and was replaced by a sense of awe and respect.

This was *his* exquisite ranch.

Eileen was wowed by what she saw, and it didn't take long for her to decide that she wanted to be a part of it. Her tour quickly took the form of an interview to become a student.

"Come along with me into the office and we can get to know each other better. I need to learn more about your disability and any possible medical issues you have to contend with before you get on a horse. Also, we'll need to make arrangements for you to get a doctor's release before you can start."

His manner was warm yet professional as he explained the requirements of the program. Commitment and punctuality were strongly emphasized.

"Students who come late or don't show are promptly dismissed. Just because lessons are offered at no cost, it doesn't mean that they don't have value," he said.

The more he told her about the requirements of the program, the more attractive the program seemed. It was clear that nothing about this was going to be easy, but she was ready for the challenge.

At the end of her lengthy interview, Eileen earned a new title.

"Dragons are the obstacles in our life, and everyone has a dragon to slay, whether it is seen or unseen," said Josef. "Even the person who appears to have everything may be struggling inside just like we are. Only with love and courage can we slay the dragon."

Eileen was now a Dragon Slayer, and, as she picked up her sword, her life began to change.

Eileen's first lesson was a week later. She left work an hour early to get to the barn on time for class.

"First things first," said Josef as they walked into the tack room. "Let's find a helmet that fits you. This will be the first thing you do every time you come for a lesson."

Eileen couldn't wait to don the smart-looking black velvet riding helmet she'd seen on English riders in horse movies and in the

Olympics. The moment she put it on, she began to feel like a real, live horsewoman. Wearing riding breaches and boots would prove too difficult for her to get on and off over the leg braces, so jeans and a smart pullover sweater or denim shirt became her typical riding attire.

She was sure that her hands would present a serious challenge. It was her biggest concern. She demonstrated to Josef that she had no ability to close her hands into a fist or grasp an object.

He smiled and said, "This is easily remedied, my dear."

He took a pair of English hunting reins and easily adapted them by making a small leather loop in each rein. These loops would enable her to hold a rein in each hand but had enough give in them so her hands wouldn't get caught in them, should she get unseated and fall off.

She was concerned that she might not have enough strength in her hands and arms to stop a horse.

"All the Dragon Slayer horses, including Scarlett, who will be your mount in the beginning, are trained to respond to voice commands," said Josef.

As she watched the other students, many of them children, she could see that he was right. Becky, a ten-year-old whose lesson time preceded hers also used loops on the reins. She was missing the lower part of her arms due to a birth defect. Eileen watched in admiration as Becky steered her horse through a pattern of poles laid out in the arena.

If she can do it, I can do it.

Josef's horses were exceptionally well-trained and hand-picked for their patience and kindness. His trust in them and confidence in their training was the added assurance she needed.

It was time to mount Scarlett, the tall bay Thoroughbred mare. Scarlett was a 16.3 hand Irish Hunter, tall even for her breed. The top of Eileen's head didn't even reach her back. Thoroughbreds are known to be energetic and, at times, a handful. But Scarlett was as patient and helpful as she was tall.

Getting on the horse required the use of a long mounting ramp and some assistance from Nancy, one of Josef's many devoted volunteers. Nancy helped guide Eileen's leg over the back of the English saddle. Just as Eileen's leg was going over Scarlett's back, the horse leaned in to close the distance.

Once seated, she felt completely at home and quickly discovered her balance on horseback was a thousand times better than her balance on the ground.

Josef was nowhere near as surprised about it.

"My dear, you were born for this," he said as she looked down at him from a height she hadn't experienced since climbing trees as a young child.

That first day he taught her the basics of walk, whoa, stand square, and back up. Then he did the thing she had been secretly hoping for.

"Nancy, would you mind opening the gate for us?" said Josef.

He set her free. Eileen and Josef rode together out of the arena and onto the wooded trail. This was one of the dreams that constantly escaped Eileen's box. The trail that led to and from the stable was one of several old logging roads that were wide enough for two riders to ride side-by-side. Eileen looked up into the canopy of the redwoods and couldn't contain the smile that lit up her face.

She glanced over her shoulder to Josef, who wore a smile of his own.

I think he knew I had been waiting for this.

They were accompanied by Nancy, also on horseback, in case an extra set of arms and legs were needed for safety. And by the end of her first lesson, this butterfly was in full-blown metamorphosis.

Once dismounted, Josef demonstrated the brushes and techniques for properly grooming a horse after a ride.

Things just keep getting better, thought Eileen.

Every grooming brush had a strap on it, so gripping the brush wasn't a problem. And with the strength she had in her upper arms, she was able to apply the proper amount of pressure with each stroke.

It was obvious that Scarlett enjoyed being groomed and it was wonderful to be able to give something back to the horse who had just taken her across the threshold into a world she'd been dreaming about since she was a child. At the end of the grooming session, she kissed Scarlett on her soft, sweet-smelling muzzle.

Eileen took off her helmet and said, "Thank you, Josef, and thank you, Nancy, for an experience that surpassed all of my expectations."

They smiled knowingly.

My next lesson day can't come fast enough!

A few weeks later, Josef introduced Eileen to the trot. Since she didn't have sufficient strength in her legs to post up and down in the saddle, she would be doing a sitting trot. Fortunately, Scarlett's movements were very smooth, and Eileen was now confident that Scarlett would stop or slow down when asked.

New skills were always taught in the arena where it was easier to keep the situation under control. Eileen's heart was thumping with excitement. She was thrilled to trot and couldn't believe how quickly and easily she advanced to this point. Most physical skills took time for her, but so far, all things horse related, she took to like a fish to water.

The younger students learned to trot at the end of a lead line or with one of the volunteers riding on the horse behind them, but Eileen's balance was secure enough to work independently at the trot. Her years of riding bareback on her Turkish neighbors' farm horses, before she had a disability, served her well and her balance on horseback was excellent.

The moment finally came when Eileen said, "And trot!"

Scarlett took off obediently. The rhythmic sound of her hoofbeats pounding across the arena in a quick pace resounded deep in Eileen's soul. She had already exceeded her own expectations of what she was capable of on horseback, but she knew there was so much more to come.

CHAPTER 7

Eileen trusted Josef completely when it came to horses, so when he suggested it was time to canter, she was willing to give it a try. However, it was hard for her to imagine that the same hands that were incapable of picking up a dime would somehow be able to control a horse at a canter, a three-beat gait that's typically faster than a trot but not quite as fast as a gallop.

"My dear, you've got excellent balance, and, if you keep in mind that Scarlett is your partner and will do what you ask of her, you'll do just fine," Josef assured.

After warming up at a walk, then at the trot, Josef gave the instructions to canter.

"Sit deep in the saddle, keep your shoulders back, and tell Scarlett to canter when you're ready."

They were moving at the trot when Eileen sung the word with as much confidence as she could muster, "Canter!"

She immediately felt the difference in Scarlett's gait. It was a surprisingly smooth rocking-horse motion, much smoother than a trot, though it covered ground much faster. Eileen was in awe watching the ground disappear under Scarlett's hooves so quickly. Josef had her work in both directions, practicing the transitions from walk, trot, canter and back again.

"What do you think?" he asked.

She smiled at him and said, "You know I can't pick up a dime, don't you?"

Smiling back, he replied, "My dear girl, you don't need to be able to pick up a dime—with four good legs beneath you and the wind in your face, there's nowhere in the world you won't be able to go from here on out!"

Her joy was apparent, and she was experiencing a level of freedom and **mobility** she hadn't known before. It was something Josef witnessed in all his students and because he, too, had a disability, he understood first-hand what this freedom meant. As an experienced horseman with a disability, he also had a keen insight into his students' capabilities. Where other instructors would focus on limitations, Josef viewed every student from the viewpoint of their potential. All his students achieved a level of success with horses that exceeded everyone else's expectations.

The freedom of movement Eileen experienced on horseback was a life-changing gift, but it wasn't the only one she'd receive by becoming a Dragon Slayer. For the first time, she began to experience a sense of community. Being around the other students with their various disabilities, all of them sharing a common love of horses and the outdoors, helped her shed her mantle of discomfort. She had never developed friendships with other people like her; it was something she had resisted since becoming disabled.

Laughter changed everything. The humorous "insider" moments helped wear away Eileen's defenses. The relationships she developed with the other students provided something that had been missing in her life. Laughing with Josef and her fellow students over the crazy circumstances that often arose from their disabilities was both liberating and bonding.

She was safe, in an accepting environment where one could laugh at oneself and poke fun at things a non-disabled person might find awkward or uncomfortable. Indeed, disability humor would become one of the arrows in her quiver and it would serve her well in the years to come.

Josef perceived her resistance to hanging out with other disabled people early on, but he never judged her for it. It was something he had seen many times before. He began addressing these delicate issues on their trail rides when it was just the two of them. The redwood forest was a safe place to discuss matters of the heart. Plus, there is something about horses that enables people to be honest and open.

"My dear, without friends who understand what it is to walk in your shoes, your life will be missing something valuable," he explained as they rode side-by-side under the canopy.

He was right, of course, but he also understood that kids growing up with disabilities face a special challenge. Not only are they different from everyone in their classroom, they're also different from their own family members as well. Most kids with physical disabilities grow up with able-bodied parents and siblings, which was certainly true for Eileen.

As a kid growing up in the 60s and 70s, there was little to no opportunity for her to interact with other kids with disabilities, and then there was the added challenge of having been able-bodied for the first eleven years of her life.

It was easy for Josef to see that she was still wrestling with self-concept, trying to figure out where and how she fit into the world as a **person with a disability**. Becoming a Dragon Slayer would change all that. Josef and the horses helped her discover that people with disabilities were her community, her people, whose friendship and support added something to her life that she never knew was missing.

The other critical element that had been missing in her life was a role model, an adult with a disability who was living an independent and fulfilling life. It's such a rarity for kids with disabilities to have access to such a person, yet it can make all the difference in the world. Josef was the first person with a disability that she had come across who was living the kind of life that she desired for herself.

With his example, she began to imagine possibilities she had never considered, like perhaps even a life that included a horse of her own. She knew there would always be obstacles, but with a powerful role model like Josef, she could now envision a future with possibilities. Even so, she wasn't prepared for what was about to happen next. It was a true exercise in dreaming big.

Chapter 8

Josef Rivers

Josef, like Merlin, was wise and well versed in science, prophecy, and wildlife. Merlin was a seer, Arthur's counselor, and according to legend, the master architect of Arthur's reign. Some say the same of Josef and Eileen.

Josef was born in England. He was from Cornwall, not far from the birthplace of King Arthur. His mother died when he was a toddler. For many years it was just Josef and his father, Walter Rivers. They became quite close. Walter worked in the Diplomatic Corps and was transferred to Bolivia when Josef was a young boy. As the child of a diplomat, he went to a private school and spent his free time enjoying a house filled with all the exotic birds and monkeys his indulgent father permitted.

Josef came from a long line of English equestrians. He learned to ride and work with horses from his father, a gifted horseman, who learned from his father before him. Walter recognized in his young son a deep passion for and a rare connection with animals, especially horses.

Despite the onset of Josef's disability at age two from polio, Walter saw no reason to coddle him and saw to it that he learned all aspects of horsemanship including riding, driving, breeding, and training in an atmosphere that was loving and supportive to horses and humans alike. The Rivers family was especially fond of the high-stepping breeds of horses and ponies one often sees on bridle paths in England. Breeds such as Hackneys, Saddlebreds, and Arabians were always a part of Rivers Crest Stables though these breeds were traditionally associated more with showing and competing than with trail riding.

By the time Eileen met Josef, he was well known in the horse community as a breeder of fine Hackneys for competitive carriage driving. In time, she would become exposed to several other breeds as well, all of which contributed to her acquiring a well-rounded experience of horses and horsemanship.

The Dragon Slayer philosophy originated with Josef's father, Walter. When Josef was young, Walter introduced him to the idea of how obstacles, like dragons, can overpower us if we let them.

"Everyone has a dragon to slay, whether visible or invisible," said Walter. "And if you don't slay the dragon, it will defeat you. Only with love and courage, only by helping others can you slay it."

This loving, fatherly wisdom became the foundation for Josef's life and one day became the foundation for Eileen's.

CHAPTER 9

The *offer* came on a trail ride through the magical redwood forest. It was just the two of them, Eileen on Scarlett and Josef on Alex, a purebred Arabian gelding. A half hour into the ride Josef turned to Eileen.

"What do you think about what I do for a job?" he asked.

"Are you kidding? I think you have a dream job!" she said.

"Do you think you could ever see yourself doing something like this?"

"If I had horses of my own, sure, I could see myself doing something like this. But I don't see how I could make that happen at this point," she said.

"Well, I want to make an offer to you, and I want you to think about it for a year before you give me your answer. I'm not going to live forever, and I would like to see this work continue. If, after a year, you think you could see yourself doing something like this, I will teach you everything I know and give you a couple of trained therapy horses so that you could go anywhere in the world and start a program of your own. It would take about seven years of commitment and hard work, which is why I don't want your answer today. There's only one condition: you must promise me that your services will always be given to your students at no charge, the way that you have received them."

Eileen's eyebrows furrowed. Not long ago, he had opened the box and let her dream fly free; now he was offering to crush the box entirely so they could never be hidden away again. He was offering her his legacy and life's work as well. But young Eileen was a suspicious creature.

What's with this guy? He barely knows me. Why on earth would he make such an offer to me? Is he a weirdo after all? Is he on the up and up?

She had to know. She had to ask, "What makes you think that you can make this type of offer to me? You've only known me for two or three months."

"You forget, my dear girl, we met many years ago, and I knew then that our paths would cross once more and that I would make you this offer."

Goosebumps crawled up Eileen's arms and the magic in the air crackled as the little hairs on her neck stood on end. This was the moment she started to believe that her newfound mentor was otherworldly.

That first encounter, years ago, lasted all of forty-five minutes, yet it was sufficient for him to know that I was the protégé he had been looking for.

Eileen went home and circled the date on her calendar so she would know when one year had passed. Three hundred and sixty-five days later, she drove to the stables, hardly able to contain herself.

"My answer is yes," said Eileen.

"Good. Now we have a great deal of work to do; let's get to it," said Josef.

There was now an increased sense of purpose in her lessons. Eager to learn more about running a stable and setting up a therapeutic riding program, Eileen arranged her schedule to accommodate two weekly lessons.

A month or so after saying yes to Josef's offer, they finished up a training session with a relaxing trail ride in the redwood forest, just the two of them. As they rode side-by-side, the conversation turned to the future.

"Have you given any thought as to what you'll call your program?" he asked.

"Actually, I've been thinking about it quite a lot," she said. "Since my program will be an offshoot of the Dragon Slayers, I think it's important for the name to have some sort of tie-in that people will instantly recognize, something that conveys romance and chivalry."

Eileen and Josef looked at each other and said simultaneously, "Camelot!"

It made perfect sense. The name Camelot has always been synonymous with people gathering at the Round Table, all rising to their highest good. King Arthur believed in **equality**. He chose a round table for his knights because there is no head, making everyone, including the king, an equal. The table represented the ideals of knighthood and chivalry. Yes, Camelot was the perfect name.

"You do know what this means, don't you?" he asked.

She thought for a moment, "No, I don't think I do. What does it mean?"

"It means that from now on I shall have to call you Wart." His smile was radiant, and his eyes sparkled with obvious pleasure.

When Arthur became Merlin's protégé, he earned a nickname: The Wart. Eileen had earned the title as well. Josef was unlike anyone she had ever met. He was indeed her Merlin, her counselor and the architect of her reign in Camelot.

CHAPTER 10

Eileen and her friends learned as much working on the ground with horses as they did from the riding lessons. This is where all the trust is established between horse and human.

"The work on the ground is every bit as important as the work in the saddle," said Josef.

He explained that physical strength has nothing to do with gaining the trust and respect of a horse. It has more to do with learning how a horse experiences the world through its senses and how they're treated.

"This can be done regardless of one's physical limitations," he assured. "If you make the effort to understand them and always treat them with kindness and respect, there's nothing a horse won't do for you."

He seemed to have an uncanny understanding of horses, a mystical connection perhaps. Eileen enjoyed observing him around the horses. Never once did she hear him raise his voice or see him strike one. Given the difficulty of Josef's gait, it would have been easy for a horse to take advantage of him on the ground, and yet, without exception, they all wanted to please him.

Clearly, physical strength isn't the key to getting a horse's cooperation. I can't wait to learn his methods.

Often, he would share this wisdom on trail rides or during hay bale chats. Josef encouraged students who drove to their lessons to stick around afterward to help feed and enjoy the ambience of the barn as the horses munched their dinner. Almost everyone was eager to get home before the traffic got heavy, but not Eileen. She craved as much time at the stable as she could get.

They'd sit on hay bales in the aisle of the barn, and she'd soak up the wisdom he shared in his elegant English accent. These hay bale chats became mentoring sessions to prepare her for establishing her own program. He covered such areas as horse evaluations, vet care, training methods, barn management, and fundraising.

"My presentations to service clubs and civic groups help raise the funds that cover the costs of the program," he said. "I call it 'keeping hay on the table'."

When he wasn't teaching, Josef spent many hours a week raising funds and community support so that students could receive their lessons at no cost.

"I can see there's a lot of work involved in keeping a program free of charge," said Eileen.

"That's quite true, but you can't put a price on freedom and dignity."

Josef used his horses as examples to teach about physical attributes, personality traits, background, and breeding. Eileen thoroughly enjoyed these sessions, especially the ones in which he discussed their idiosyncrasies and herd dynamics. Horses were endlessly fascinating to her.

Weather permitting, the horses were turned out together in the arena for the evening. Josef and Eileen spent many sunsets simply watching them interact, entertained by the thought of what they might be saying to each other.

He also covered how to assess students, beginning with their disabilities, comfort level around horses, ability to follow instructions, and possible medical conditions (even though not every disability is considered a medical condition). He stressed the importance of remembering each person's dignity, always.

While his lessons with Eileen carried extra weight, each of his students received an all-encompassing education in horsemanship. Regardless of age or disability, they were required to learn horse anatomy, how to take care of horses, the various saddles and tack used in riding or working with horses, and safety practices.

Everyone was also given the opportunity to try their hand at driving ponies and horses. They began by learning with the Shetland ponies. Some students progressed to the larger ponies and, in some cases, full-sized horses.

There were several different types of carts and carriages at the ranch, including the lightweight, two-wheeled pleasure carts often seen at racetracks and the fancy velvet-seated Viceroy, designed for the showier breeds like Hackneys, Arabians, and Saddlebreds.

Eileen gobbled it all up!

The entry to the ranch property included a hard-packed dirt driveway that encircled the stable and arena, making it easier for horse trailers to enter and exit the property. It also served as a great track for learning to drive a cart or carriage. All driving lessons began in the arena with Josef or one of his assistants in the cart next to the student driver. Once it was established that they could control the pony at the trot (cantering is never permitted in pleasure driving), adult students were allowed to drive independently on the circular dirt drive with Josef watching and coaching from his usual observation point. Ever mindful of safety, he placed one or two volunteers at intervals in between, just in case.

Eileen took to driving with ease. It offered an altogether different experience than riding. It was like being in a convertible car, only better. With loops on the driving reins, she was able to steer and stop a horse in harness every bit as well as in the saddle. She relished the beauty of the scenery passing by at a relaxing pace as well as the gentle sway of the horse's tail keeping time with the delightful clippety-clop of hooves on the track—the latter a favorite for the visually impaired students.

Before long, Josef felt her skill level was sufficient to enter a local horse show that included pleasure driving classes. Her first time in the show ring was with Henry, a stout Shetland pony with flaxen mane and tail. Henry had very nice driving manners, which made her look good. She was more than thrilled when the judge announced their number as the third-place winner of the class.

The opportunity to work with different breeds of horses with different gaits, as well as learning to drive, added to her growing level of skill and confidence. Exposing his students to different horses and equipment was Josef's way of teaching them that their skills were not dependent on one particular horse or saddle.

Through the medium of horsemanship, Josef taught life lessons. His approach was both accepting and challenging. He accepted her for who she was but always saw her as she could be. Never once did he let her forget that she was someone who had enormous potential, a message she had never heard prior to this. He used every lesson to convey to her that she could be, or do, anything that she wanted, just like anyone else. In fact, she had a *responsibility* to be, or do, all that she could.

But the most important lesson of all, a lesson that he reminded her of every day was this: "The more you share, the more you'll have. Kindness and generosity are the keys to being a success."

CHAPTER 11

From day one, Eileen was curious about the beautiful sidesaddle in the corner of the tack room. She'd never seen one before, except in movies, and couldn't imagine how women kept their balance, especially at a trot or a canter. This saddle looked slightly different than movie sidesaddles because it had a single horn, instead of a double, also known as a leaping horn.

"This saddle is designed for pleasure riding as opposed to hunting and going over jumps," explained Josef.

"How do people keep their balance riding sidesaddle?" Eileen asked.

"It's not as difficult as one might think," he said. "In fact, I think you might like it if you give it a try. Many able-bodied riders find the idea of riding sidesaddle intimidating because both the rider's legs are on the same side of the horse. They feel this would affect their balance and limit their ability to communicate with their horse through their legs.

"But someone with a disability that affects their legs often does very well riding sidesaddle because they are not dependent on the use of their legs for their balance or their communication with a horse. You, for instance, have natural balance on a horse, which comes from your seat, not your legs. Just wait till you try it," he said with a twinkle in his eye.

A few weeks after that conversation, Eileen arrived at her usual lesson time and saw the sidesaddle on its stand in the aisle of the barn, next to where Scarlett was tied. Nancy stood by smiling. She'd been waiting a long time to see a student learn to ride sidesaddle, and on this lovely day in 1977, she got her wish.

Josef tacked up, paying close attention to how the saddle was aligned on the horse's back so that the rider's weight would be evenly distributed. All the while, he explained the proper position for the rider's body and legs.

"All future lessons in the sidesaddle will be conducted with you in a dress," he said in his proper English accent.

Oh boy, that means I'll need to go shopping at the local vintage clothing stores to find a long dress with a full enough skirt to cover both legs while in the saddle.

The mounting process was tricky, but with Nancy's help, she was able to get situated in the saddle with her right leg wrapped around the horn. A sidesaddle has no stirrup for the right leg, yet once she was properly seated, she felt surprisingly secure. Josef was right once again: she had no hesitation about having both her legs on the same side of the horse.

I guess my disability can be an asset instead of an obstacle at times.

If she was properly seated, aligning her spine with the horse's spine, riding sidesaddle was a cinch. Eileen looked down at her and Scarlett's shadow on the ground.

"Well, don't we look elegant."

This was an eye-opener, another way for her to see herself, and for a change, she really liked what she saw. The more experience she gained with horses, the more her self-acceptance and self-confidence grew.

Scarlett was a perfect sidesaddle mount with her tall, elegant frame and her comfortable gaits. It also helped that she was so responsive to verbal cues. Eileen didn't need a crop or anything else to get her to walk or trot. On a smooth gaited horse, trotting sidesaddle was no different than trotting astride.

Josef enjoyed watching her succeed at riding sidesaddle as much as Eileen was enjoying it herself. She found a couple of nice vintage dresses and always showed up properly attired for a sidesaddle lesson.

After only a few classes Josef said, "Are you ready to try cantering sidesaddle?"

I do feel secure up here.

"Sure!"

He had her ride to a particular portion of the circular trail that wound around the ranch because it had an incline.

"You'll feel more secure going uphill in the beginning than cantering on a flat trail," said Josef. Then he positioned himself at the top of the hill, knowing that if she somehow lost control of the horse, Scarlett would stop right in front of him.

"When you're ready, give her a cluck and tell her to canter," he said.

She clucked and said with emphasis, "Canter!"

And then, as if in a dream, Eileen effortlessly cantered up the trail with her dress flowing and the wind rushing through her hair. She managed to bring Scarlett to a graceful halt just in front of Josef, who beamed at her with obvious pleasure and satisfaction. He'd had the sidesaddle custom made several years ago and had been waiting ever since for a student who would take to it.

Never in my wildest dreams did I imagine myself riding a sidesaddle!

It was a marvelous feeling to have mastered a skill that many able-bodied riders would find challenging. After additional work at the canter, she discovered that the security she felt in sidesaddle was because her lower legs didn't flop or bounce as they did when she cantered astride.

Josef noticed it too.

One afternoon, he told her about an upcoming horse show in the San Jose area, which included a sidesaddle class.

"The show ring is not Scarlett's cup of tea," he explained. "If you'd like to enter this show, we'll need to get you working with a different horse."

He suggested Cameo, a lovely black Tennessee Walker mare who was somewhat new to the stable. Tennessee Walkers are world famous for their smooth, gliding gaits and Cameo was no exception.

Eileen had about a month to prepare for the show with Cameo. Joanne, one of the volunteers who was a handy seamstress, made a beautiful white chiffon dress for her. Joanne also found a wide-brimmed white hat to which she attached some chiffon streamers to catch the breeze when they trotted. The white costume on the black mare guaranteed they'd catch the judge's eye.

Show day finally arrived. Sarah, a high school student who had lost her leg to childhood cancer, had also signed up for the show. She would be driving one of the ponies in a pleasure driving class. Several other Dragon Slayers were coming along to be a cheering section for those who entered in classes.

Whenever they attended horse shows as a group, they always drew a great deal of attention from other exhibitors and spectators who probably found it difficult to imagine that people with disabilities would also be interested in or knowledgeable about horses. Many of them had never interacted with a disabled person, which is why it was so important for the Dragon Slayers to be there, whether they won their class or not.

Volunteers Nancy and Joanne helped get the equipment and horses loaded in the truck and horse trailer. It was a fun ride to the Santa Clara County Fairgrounds. When they arrived, the place was buzzing with activity as people got themselves, their equipment, and their horses ready. Mounting was even more challenging when away from the ranch, but with a portable mounting block and lots of help, Eileen was able to get on Cameo. Mounting wasn't exactly elegant, but when she entered the show arena on the beautiful black mare, neither the spectators in the grandstands nor the judges had any idea that under her white chiffon gown were leg braces.

The show grounds were in the flight path of the San Jose airport. The aircraft coming in for a landing frequently passed overhead. Most of the horses were okay with this but Cameo found it unsettling. She became fussy in the show ring, backing up and attempting to get away from the noise. She wasn't responding to Eileen's verbal cues, and, without a riding crop, Eileen had no way of urging the horse forward. Eileen could see that Cameo's distress was beginning to distract the other horses, which meant she had a decision to make.

Horse show etiquette stipulates that any rider whose horse is acting up is expected to excuse herself from the arena so as not to upset the other horses and riders. And that's what she did. Even though Eileen didn't get to finish her class, the spectators gave her a standing ovation, applauding her good sportsmanship.

It wasn't the outcome she expected, but it gave her more valuable experience. She was happy things went much better for Sarah, who went on to take second place in her driving class. It was a victory for all the Dragon Slayers.

Eileen continued riding sidesaddle for other occasions, including the local parade. The Dragon Slayers always had a colorful entry, which included several of the younger students riding in costume in a decorated horse-drawn wagon with Josef at the reins. She was proud to be part of the unit riding sidesaddle in period costumes.

Eileen had finally come off the sidelines of life. She was no longer a spectator hoping to someday be included as an equal. She was part of something big—something much bigger than herself.

CHAPTER 12

Eileen graduated college in August of 1977 and immediately started job hunting in the field of social services. She applied for lots of jobs with various agencies and programs, including group homes for at-risk youth. During interviews, she was constantly asked questions about her physical limitations instead of her experience, talents, or abilities. These questions would not be permitted today as they are considered discriminatory, but this was well before the ADA, so qualified job applicants who happened to have disabilities had to contend with negative reactions from would-be employers over and over. Eileen was passed over for everything she applied for and became profoundly discouraged.

Getting hired for her first professional job after college would involve overcoming multiple barriers. There were physical barriers, also known as **architectural barriers**, such as stairs at building entrances. But worse yet were the **attitude barriers** she encountered during interviews; for example, when someone assumes that a person with a disability is somehow inferior or incapable or that someone with a speech impairment can't understand what other people are saying to them. Attitude barriers develop when people form ideas about a person because of **stereotypes** or a lack of knowledge; they're often more difficult to overcome than physical ones.

She attended interview after interview without success. Josef, the horses, and the friendships she had developed with the other Dragon Slayers were the best part of that frustrating year. Her lessons often came on the heels of another disappointing job interview.

Josef sensed her frustration, and, on those days, he would say, "Go out into the redwoods and let your horse solve your problem for you."

Riding in the forest always restored her serenity. Everything was green and soft. Decades-old, fallen logs were covered in moss while graceful ferns lined the banks of the trail. Sound was muted by the soft, fragrant soil under her horse's feet. Only the breeze through the trees, an occasional blue jay, and the creaking of saddle leather permeated the silence. The forest was a sacred space for her; she envisioned it to be a green cathedral. These quiet rides, alone with nature, never failed to uplift her.

One of her favorite spots in the redwood forest was where the creek crossed the trail. It was about fifteen feet across and about a foot down at its deepest point. The water was clear enough to see minnows and the occasional crawdad. Some horses don't like walking in flowing water but that wasn't the case with any of the Dragon Slayer horses.

Eileen was always grateful to Scarlett, who walked ever so politely through the sparkling water, enabling her to experience a world she would never have access to on foot. While every inch of the redwood forest was breathtakingly beautiful, most of it was not accessible to her were it not for a good horse.

One afternoon, Josef told Eileen and the other Dragon Slayers about an opportunity to earn the Presidential Sports Award. This was not an award specific to people who had disabilities, but rather a nationwide program sponsored by the President's Council on Physical Fitness to encourage people to get out and be active. It was open to athletes of all ages and all disciplines, from power walking or track to swimming, hiking, boating, and even equitation.

Earning the patch required a minimum of fifty hours of supervised (so nobody could cheat) physical activity to be completed in a four-month period. Each session would count for one hour toward the total. In other words, spending three hours on a hike or a trail ride would only count as one hour toward the fifty-hour goal. This meant that Eileen would need to ride at least three times per week for the next four months. She was certainly more than willing to do so, and it would give her something positive to work toward while continuing to search for a job.

Her regular weekly lesson counted toward one of the hours. She racked up the other two hours per week by riding the forest trails. Sometimes she rode with friends who were also working toward their patch, but many times she rode alone. Since Eileen required assistance with her mount and dismount, this was acceptable as a "supervised" activity.

Eileen wasn't afraid to ride alone. She accepted the fact that, sooner or later, every serious horse person is going to fall off. Falling and learning to get back up is a part of life, with or without horses. Eileen believed as Josef believed—that denying people with disabilities the opportunity to explore risk is denying them one of their basic human rights. Josef understood the importance of people with disabilities being allowed to test their abilities and explore risk. And, as a disabled horseman himself, he understood from his own experience that people with disabilities are capable of so much more than meets the eye. He had every confidence that she could handle herself and her horse, come what may.

On one occasion, Eileen did fall off her horse while riding alone. She was riding Countess when a jogger came out of nowhere, scaring her horse and causing the mare to jump sideways. This unexpected movement caused Eileen to lose her seat and land unceremoniously on the soft soil. The jogger felt terrible, but Eileen assured him she was okay and waved him on.

"Go home, girl," she said to Countess knowing that the trail would lead the horse back to the stable.

Twenty minutes later Josef and Nancy appeared on horseback with Countess in tow. They were able to assist Eileen in getting re-mounted and the three of them enjoyed the rest of the trail ride together. The incident and the way she handled it solidified in the minds of both teacher and student that Eileen was capable of getting unseated and handling the experience properly.

At the end of four months, she easily acquired the fifty hours needed to earn her patch. In 1978, she held the certificate and the beautiful Presidential Patch for Equitation and smiled. It was particularly gratifying to know that no one on the Presidential Sports Award committee knew of her disability. She competed on even ground with everyone else. This was a milestone she would cherish forever.

A few months later, Eileen finally landed a job in a social service agency, the Skills Center of Santa Cruz. She wouldn't be working with at-risk youth as she had hoped. Her title was program manager, but her duties were those of a social worker for adults with intellectual disabilities. It wasn't her first choice for a job; it wasn't even her fifth. Even though she was grateful for the work, she was aggravated that the only place that would hire her was a place for people with disabilities.

Yet, once again, she landed exactly where she needed to be for that time in her life. She developed several lifelong friendships, including friendships with other young adults with disabilities. She learned a great deal about how to be an **advocate** for herself and for others. She also learned how **nonprofit organizations** work and the value they contribute to their communities. The job she didn't think she would enjoy proved to be the best springboard for the program she wanted to start, the program that would become her life's work.

CHAPTER 13

Eileen always had a deep connection with animals, two in particular; one had hooves and the other had wings. Her lifelong appreciation of birds deepened when she was in the hospital as a child. These days, children's hospitals in the U.S. do their best to make sure their young patients are comfortable and entertained. But when Eileen was hospitalized, they were stark places that focused solely on medical needs, not needs of the heart and soul.

Birds were a rare source of joy. Even pigeons, which were typically pegged as pests, were welcomed at her window. Her body may have been stuck in a bed for the time being, but her imagination was free, dancing on the windowsill with her feathered friends, nesting in the rafters, and flying in the sky. Her love of birds made Josef's gift even more exceptional.

One spring afternoon in 1980, Josef asked Eileen to take home a juvenile Chinese Gray goose who was only a few months old. He wanted her to gentle the bird for the upcoming Dragon Slayer summer camp. Although the goose's body was nearly adult sized, she was still in the squeaking and humming phase of her communication.

As with chickens, ducks, and other barnyard fowl, the baby goose emerges from the egg peeping. Within a few days that peep turns into a "cheep". As the gosling loses its baby fuzz, the cheep becomes more of a squeak and an occasional hum, which reflects curiosity or contentment, depending on the circumstances. They don't honk until they reach a certain age.

"I don't know what to name her," said Eileen.

"My dear, one does not give a goose a name. Rather, it is the goose who reveals its name in its own good time," said Josef.

The first thing to know about a goose is that they are wise and brave. It's the goose who's the boss of the barnyard. There are no Mother Chicken nursery rhymes nor Mother Pig or Mother Duck nursery rhymes. Mother Goose rules.

Eileen was now renting the lower half of a split-level home with a fenced-in, terraced garden—a fine place for housing a goose. She took the young goose home in the new little pickup truck she'd purchased to fit her increasingly horsey lifestyle, and they began to get to know each other. Like all geese, this one had lots to say. The two of them had many lively conversations throughout the day. When Eileen worked, the goose would spend her time in Eileen's beautiful backyard garden, bathing in her tub or meandering through the raised flowerbeds, eating bugs and eliminating every weed in sight. Geese are helpful that way. Unlike a chicken, a goose doesn't eat the flowering plants, only the weeds that pop up.

In the evenings, Eileen would go out and sit with her on the concrete steps between the flower beds. The goose would always come over and stand on her lap with her beautiful orange webbed feet, squeaking her comments about her day and humming her deep satisfaction at having a beautiful place to live as well as a companion who cherished her. Since Eileen didn't yet know her name, she called her "Goose-goose" to which she always responded with a squeak or a hum.

Geese are sticklers for following rules and observing schedules, another trait that makes them great barnyard bosses. Their pleasant little life in the garden followed the same pattern nearly every day. One evening, after the goose had been with Eileen for about three or four weeks, Eileen went out into the garden to be with her and watch the sunset. As was her custom, the goose climbed onto Eileen's lap the moment she sat down on the steps.

It was a beautiful evening; the temperature was mild enough for Eileen to stay out with her until after dark. It was a clear night, and, together, they watched the stars emerge, conversing in the language they both understood.

"So, what is your name, my friend?" Eileen asked her.

The goose looked Eileen in the face with her beautiful dark eyes, then turned and looked upward at the stars.

"Are you telling me the answer is up there?"

The goose continued to gaze upward, so Eileen followed her line of sight as best she could. Directly above them was a constellation she couldn't name, but the brightest of its stars were aligned in a "Z".

"Is Zanadu your name?"

"Squeak, squeak, squonk, hooonk, hooonk!" the goose answered enthusiastically.

Thus, Zanadu revealed her name.

Needless to say, Zanadu never moved back to Josef's barn.

"Keep her as your companion goose and yard protector," said Josef upon seeing their mutual devotion.

The bond between the young goose and Eileen was strong, but it would be tested before the year was over.

Josef was full of surprises. He also brought on Guenivere and a couple of other new horses that summer. Scarlett was in her early twenties and starting to experience arthritis. Having faithfully served a generation of Dragon Slayers, Josef felt she was entitled to retirement in a lush pasture. Guenivere was one of the horses who would assume many of Scarlett's duties as a school horse.

She was a palomino, with a Quarter Horse type of build, medium height and stocky. She was a quiet horse, unassuming, nothing flashy except her color. Without a pedigree, Guinevere was considered a grade horse. Grade horses, while not commanding the prices of purebreds, are still worth their weight in gold as lesson horses. Most of them are the result of crossbreeding, which often ends up producing horses with great temperaments and highly desirable physical attributes—qualities that are highly sought after in lesson horses.

Guenevere was an excellent example of a grade horse. She was sturdy, as easy going and patient as they come, and also forgiving. She always did whatever was asked of her, taking everything in her stride. After working with her off-and-on for the next year or so, Josef and Eileen began to regard her as a potential school horse for a fledgling program. Eileen's program.

Zanadu was stolen from their beautiful, backyard garden on Thanksgiving Day of that year. Eileen couldn't help but imagine the worst: could somebody have stolen her goose for their Thanksgiving meal? She searched every puddle, lake, and body of water in Santa Cruz for three months to no avail.

...AND
SHE
FLEW

The Grand Canyon

The finest armor in the realm will be for naught if thou hast not a horse that is sure of foot and stout of heart. ~Unknown

CHAPTER 14

Eileen had been working at the Skills Center for nearly three years and had developed lasting friendships with several of her co-workers. Her friend Mark was still working there. But he was transferred to another department where he taught money skills to the adult clientele. It was a close-knit staff, and many of them shared a love of the outdoors. Mark often organized weekend camping trips to Big Sur; it was one of Eileen's favorite adventures with the trusted group.

One day, Pam, one of her closest work friends, invited Eileen to join her the following summer on her Grand Canyon trip. "My sister, Debbie, and brother-in-law, Clay, and their kids from Colorado are all coming," Pam told her. They were all seasoned hikers and campers. "You'll fit right in!"

Eileen had seen much of the world outside the United States but had only visited Grand Canyon through pages of National Geographic magazine. Seeing this natural wonder with her friend sounded like the vacation of a lifetime. The two friends hatched a plan in which Pam and her family would hike down and camp, while

Eileen would take the world-famous mule ride down to the bottom. The pamphlets they received from Grand Canyon National Park recommended reservations for camping and mule rides be made at least six months in advance.

No problem.

In January, Eileen called the park and made her reservations, convinced her years in the saddle made her more than qualified to ride a mule.

The redwood trees of northern California were replaced by junipers, ponderosas, and cacti. The moist oceanic air turned dry long before Eileen and her two friends neared their destination in the heart of Arizona: the Grand Canyon. A month or so before their departure, Pam asked if it would be okay for her boyfriend to come along. Richard, who also worked at the Skills Center, had a great sense of humor and was fun to be around. Plus, it would be great to have a third person to share the long drive. They spent months preparing for this trip to one of the seven natural wonders of the world. The timing was perfect. Early summer would bring warm days and cool nights at the South Rim.

The friends did their research. The canyon was between four to eighteen miles across depending on where you stood. It was two hundred and seventy-seven miles long and a mile deep in some places. The Colorado River carves through the canyon: a six-million-year-old work of art in the making, sliced like a multi-colored cake with shades of reds, hues of purple, creamy orange, chocolate, and creams. Layers of sandstone, mudstone, shale, igneous, and sedimentary rocks made up its colorful layers.

Much of the canyon is managed by the park service, so Eileen figured the paths and exhibits near the touristy South Rim would be well maintained and accessible. Eileen's friends were all able-bodied. Pam, Richard, Debbie, her husband Clay, and their kids had reservations to hike down to the bottom of the canyon and camp for three days before hiking back out. Eileen was looking forward to riding down on a mule. Since the rest of the group would be on a three-day expedition and the mule ride would only be a one-day affair, she planned on taking advantage of the shuttle buses and guided tours to see as much of the canyon from the rim as possible before her friends returned.

The strong and surefooted mules at the canyon have carved their way through history like the river. They were first used by early prospectors in the area and became an option for tourists in the 1880s. They're ideal to ride on the steep, narrow path to and from the canyon's bottom. Eileen had read the mule ride rules carefully before even setting a date for their trip. She was tall enough. Check. She was well under their weight limit. Check. She could understand English. Check. Check. Check. The mules regularly carried visitors with no mule or horse experience. Eileen had tons.

She had been Josef's student for five years and was officially his protégé and apprentice instructor. Eileen's plans to start her own riding program were well underway. Josef had dubbed her The Wart. She was after all, his King Arthur in the making, destined to be a queen in her own right. Eileen knew she wanted acreage in a warm weather area, and she even had a name picked out for her riding program: Camelot. There was still one big question mark in her plans. Where she would build her queendom.

Josef assured her, "When the time is right, you will know."

The group rose with the sun and arrived at the mule barn early to start their adventure into the belly of the canyon. Spirits were high after much planning and many miles traveled for this experience. The start to the mule ride began at the staging area behind the famous Bright Angel Lodge located in Grand Canyon Village at the top of the rim. It was run by the Fred Harvey Company, the same company that built the original mule barn, along with the livery stable, blacksmith smithy, and saddle shop in 1906, providing services for guests of the El Tovar Hotel. When the horse-drawn carriage ride was discontinued in the 1920s, they began offering mule rides into the canyon.

Eileen took her place in the long line at the reservations counter for the mule rides. Judging by the dozens of people in line with her, she guessed this was one of the most popular activities at the park.

"Hi, I'm here for my mule ride reservation," Eileen said when she finally reached the reservations clerk, a young woman wearing the familiar Fred Harvey Company blazer and skirt.

Her eyes landed on Eileen's crutches. She could practically read her mind by the discomfort on her face.

"Don't worry. I have years of horse experience," she said, hoping to put the young woman's mind at ease. Also hoping to avoid a lengthy interaction that would undoubtedly frustrate the people standing in line behind her.

The woman shook her head and avoided eye contact, "We have a policy. People who have a handicap aren't permitted to ride the mules."

She pointed to an official-looking piece of paper under the glass counter, and there it was. On official letterhead with the Fred Harvey Company logo on top was the policy which read: No one with a physical handicap will be allowed to ride the mules.

It was as blunt as a bucket of cold water in the face.

The ADA wasn't in place in 1981, but Eileen was fully aware of the Rehabilitation Act of 1973, specifically Section 504, which prohibits any government program or any private company doing business with the government from discriminating against people with disabilities. She had rights. Legally, she could demand the opportunity to demonstrate her riding skills. She knew she would pass with flying colors.

Eileen narrowed her eyes as she weighed her options. She was frustrated with the reservations clerk and angry about the situation, but she also knew that the young woman was following orders and would probably get in trouble if she allowed Eileen to ride. Still, it was humiliating to be told no in front of all the people in line behind her, as if she were a disobedient child. Even though it was wrong any way she weighed it, this problem didn't start with the person in front of her. It started layers above.

"We aren't going to go if you can't go," said Richard. "It's not fair for you to have to stay behind while we all get to see the inner canyon."

"Please, I want you to go. And I expect good stories when you get back." She tried to smile around the lump in her throat and fought to control the familiar, sick feeling that accompanied this type of judgment. But Eileen had grown so much from the days where she'd accept the limitations people put on her.

The determined gleam returned to her green eyes and the corner of her lips raised in a genuine smile, "Don't worry. There's plenty to do around here." She reassured her friends.

The next morning Eileen dropped her friends off at the trailhead, then drove off to find a quiet spot along the rim where she could spend a few minutes feeling sorry for herself and then figure out what the heck to do over the next three days. But she hit a snag. Several snags. It didn't take long for her to realize there were more issues than the mule ride.

Wheelchairs couldn't be maneuvered down any of the canyon trails. In fact, they couldn't be wheeled into many of the buildings! The park trails and exhibits were designed for people who could see, hear, and walk, and the buildings were just as inaccessible. So were the shuttle buses and tour buses. Each barrier encountered brought an ever-increasing sense of frustration and injustice, not just for her, but for all people with disabilities who came to the park. Suddenly, it was if she felt a divine finger tapping her on the shoulder, saying, "Eileen, there's work to be done here."

The next day, Eileen returned to Bright Angel Lodge. The reservations clerk from the previous day was back on duty.

"It's me again," she greeted the young woman with a smile. "Don't worry, I'm not here to ask to ride the mules, but I am here to talk about your discriminatory policy. I know you don't make the rules, and I know that your manager doesn't make the rules, so what I'm asking of you is to put me in touch with your boss's boss. Who would that be?"

"That would be Mr. Jan Cutler. He's the director of transportation for the Fred Harvey Company."

"Would you please get him on the phone for me? I don't have much to do right now so I'm happy to wait for as long as it takes," she said as politely as she could. She knew that being respectful would bring about better results.

The young woman went to her boss, who, in turn, put in the call. It turned out to be a pleasant exchange in which Jan Cutler suggested they meet for breakfast at the lodge the next day and Eileen agreed.

The morning sun drenched yellow-orange rays over the little town on the rim, casting shadows through the trees on the paths. Eileen heaved a deep sigh as she looked up at the five concrete steps she needed to climb in order to make it to the lodge's restaurant. She mentally added this entrance to the many things she would bring up to Mr. Cutler as she carefully and painstakingly maneuvered each step.

It was risky business to attempt stairs on crutches, but she went for it by leaning back and throwing her right leg up on the step above, hoping she didn't miss. Then she pushed the rest of her body up onto the step using the crutches and repeated the exhausting process for each successive step, all while trying not to lose her balance.

"Does this table work for you?" Jan Cutler asked, motioning to a table close by. He was a tall man in his mid-40s, dressed in a business suit. Jan was much warmer and easier to talk to than Eileen expected.

Eileen wasted no time in getting to the point. "Don't worry. I don't intend to sue, but others likely will if you don't revise your policy," said Eileen. She wanted to make clear that she was interested in bringing about change, not filing a lawsuit.

He nodded as she spoke, appreciating her understanding of the issues involved, whether it was disability civil rights or liability issues facing businesses. Eileen was uplifted when she realized she was speaking with someone who was open-minded. They discussed how Section 504 applied to his operation as a company doing business with the federal government and how so many of the amenities at Grand Canyon were inaccessible. She convinced him that the mule ride policy could be rewritten in a way that did not discriminate or increase the liability for the Fred Harvey Company.

"There are some people in park management that I think need to meet you," Jan said while glancing at his watch. "I'd like you to come with me to a manager's meeting between park service and the concessionaires that run the hotels and businesses. It's taking place in about an hour. I think they need to hear what you have to say."

"I'd love to!" she said. In her mind she could hear the creak of another door opening.

After a long talk and a good breakfast, Jan took Eileen to the managers' meeting held in a conference room at the Visitor Center, where he introduced her to several park service officials, including Karen Berggren, their special populations coordinator. Karen was particularly excited to meet Eileen.

"We've been looking for someone like you for a long time," she said. After the meeting, Karen, in turn, introduced Eileen to J.T. Reynolds. He was the training manager for ranger activities at Horace M. Albright Training Center, which encompassed law enforcement, search and rescue, emergency management, structural and wild land fire protection, visitor resources, and natural and cultural resources.

"Would you consider putting together a training seminar to discuss accessibility issues and disability rights for our fall Ranger Skills course in October? We'd bring you on as a paid consultant," said J.T. As an African American park ranger and manager in the early 1980s, he too was breaking down barriers in his own right.

Eileen went to the Grand Canyon to ride a mule and soak in the sights but left as the newest presenter for the Albright Training Center.

CHAPTER 15

Eileen couldn't wait to tell Josef about the invitation from NPS to present a training on disability issues. There was something else she was eager to share.

"I get the sense that Arizona could very well be the place where I establish Camelot," she said.

Although there was nothing more than an invitation to teach the seminar in the fall, Josef felt as she did.

"Camelot isn't coming, my dear," he said prophetically, "It's *here!* We need to decide which horses you'll take with you to Arizona."

October brought the bite of fall to Santa Cruz, along with thick clouds and the promise of rain. Eileen was taking care of the final details before her second trip to Grand Canyon. In three days, she'd hit the road again, this time by herself. It was the weekend, and she had just finished putting the finishing touches on her outline for the half-day training session she would be presenting. As she packed up the handouts and the audiovisual materials she would be using in the training, she said a silent prayer that her presentation would be a success.

"If this goes well, there's a possibility I might be offered a bigger opportunity, and, if it doesn't go well—," she was afraid to consider the possibilities. She realized either would test her mettle. What she needed was to take a drive to Schwan Lake. It was her happy place and her favorite spot to recharge. She drove down East Cliff Drive and found her usual parking spot on the edge of Schwan Lake. It was technically a lagoon that was a well-known bird sanctuary near the beach. She had searched that pond a million times in hopes of finding Zanadu.

In a gaggle of white geese by the lagoon was one that stood out amongst the rest, a Chinese Gray. It was unusual to see one here.

Eileen's breath hitched as she quickly got out of the truck. The goose was in poor shape. She had a droopy wing, a pitted beak, and ragged plumage, all signs of a goose that had been in a life-or-death struggle.

Eileen hesitated a moment, considering the possibility that this sad goose was not her Zanadu.

"Goose-Goose? Is that you?" she called.

Recognition flickered in the wise bird's eyes and Eileen's doubt fizzled away like sea foam. She scanned the area for help because she couldn't scoop the goose up while standing with her crutches, and if she went to the ground, she couldn't stand up with the large bird in her arms.

Eileen walked up to two nearby fishermen. "Could you please help me? I need help getting my goose in the truck. She's been missing, and I can't do it on my own." The look of doubt in their eyes before they spoke prompted her to add, "I promise it's safe."

The fishermen shrugged. "Sure, we'll help."

The white geese waddled away as the three of them slowly walked up to the gray goose. "All you need to do is put your arms around her wings and support her feet," said Eileen. "I promise there will be no fight."

As promised, the goose didn't struggle. The fisherman with the goose in his arms followed Eileen to her little blue pickup truck. She opened the door and he carefully set the bird down. The goose made herself comfortable in the middle of the bench.

Eileen thanked the fishermen and bid her new friends farewell before getting into the truck herself. On the off chance that this bird might not be Zanadu, Eileen decided to make certain before starting the engine. In the small cab of her pickup, the five-foot wingspan of a panicking goose would surely cause an accident.

She looked at the goose, "So this is me. Is this you?"

Eileen put her arm around her. The goose put her head on Eileen's shoulder and hummed as only a happy goose can. Zanadu, the goose who chose her name by starlight was finally back home. Finding her lost goose was all the message she needed. The Universe made it clear: seemingly impossible things can happen. She was convinced that some great opportunity would emerge from her upcoming presentation at Albright Training Center, and she would say yes.

Eileen and Josef visited before her trip to Arizona, solving the problems of the world as they often did. There were only days before Eileen was scheduled to leave for the Grand Canyon.

"I have a strong feeling that a large opportunity will present itself on this trip," she told Josef.

"Funny you should say that. I have the same feeling," he said with a smile. "And I have a gift for you."

Josef handed a loosely wrapped package to Eileen.

"What beautiful wrapping!" she said as she accepted it. Josef loved giving thoughtful gifts out of the blue. He also loved receiving them and believed one should never respond by saying, "You didn't have to do that."

Her breath caught in her throat as she saw the beautifully bound and illustrated version of *Cyrano de Bergerac* from her favorite antique bookstore. She'd had her eye on it for a while.

How did he know this?

He was full of surprises. She reverently opened the cover to find Josef had inscribed it with a verse:

"Come to the edge," he said.
They said, "We are afraid."
"Come to the edge," he said.
They came. He pushed them…and they flew.

His inscription was adapted from a poem by Guillaume Apollinaire. It spoke to her of risk. Her right to risk and to embrace her dreams. These words would follow her always.

Eileen made plans for her friend Pam to be a goose sitter so Zanadu could stay in her backyard and enjoy her garden and favorite water feature. Eileen was worried about leaving so soon after finding Zanadu, but she knew this trip was important.

"I will be gone for less than a week," she told Zanadu as they sat in the garden, enjoying the stars well into the night.

A day later, Eileen set off for the Grand Canyon in her little pickup truck with only a few butterflies in her stomach to keep her company. The nerves weren't because of the drive, although the two-day solo trip probably should have concerned her more. They were due to the unshakable feeling that something big was going to happen.

For the next two days, she was completely untethered, alone with her thoughts and the road ahead. Most people didn't have mobile phones yet, and she didn't have a car phone. There were pay phones in the occasional small town she drove through, but they were useless to her. She couldn't pick up coins to deposit in the slot to place a call. And even though she couldn't pop the hood of her truck or use a tire jack for a flat tire, she felt invincible.

Zanadu was home, safe. She smiled. *Let's see what's around the corner.*

Chapter 16

Eileen stood in front of a roomful of rangers at Albright Training Academy. They came from different parks from across the United States. Eileen saw it for what it was, an opportunity to change attitudes on a broad scale. Karen had been a great sport about rounding up all the equipment in preparation for the training. At the back of the classroom were five empty wheelchairs, several pairs of crutches, and a box containing blindfolds and earplugs.

J.T. gave her a brief introduction, then turned the room over to Eileen.

"It's not our body that handicaps us, it's our environment," she began, noting a few curious expressions and some heads nodding.

Good. I have their attention.

After a brief description of her own experience as a park visitor, she said, "The issues of accessibility and disability rights are a matter of importance to everyone. Disability is the only minority group that anyone can join at any time. Any one of us, regardless of age, gender, or economic status could have an illness or accident resulting in lifelong disability. Let's begin by examining the language people commonly use when talking about disabilities or handicaps. Words are important. The words we use reflect our attitudes, especially when describing other groups of people."

She went over to the blackboard where Karen had written a list of commonly used terms. Some were respectful, and others were outdated and offensive. Hoping to inspire an honest and open discussion, she made sure the list included words like *crippled*, *lame* and *spaz*. She was pleased with the lively discussion that followed.

"I grew up hearing the word 'crippled'," said an older ranger who had grown up during the polio epidemic. Several rangers nodded in agreement. The word "crippled" was now considered stigmatizing and negative.

Another ranger said, "I was taught it was rude to acknowledge a person's disability, so my family and I simply referred to it as 'a condition'."

From somewhere in the back of the room, a ranger raised his hand. "I have a younger brother with cerebral palsy, and he was constantly being referred to by other kids as 'a spaz'. My brother is a great person, and I was prepared to beat up any kid I heard using that word."

From there, they went on to talk about **People First Language**, which emphasizes the person instead of the condition.

"For example," Eileen explained, "I don't refer to myself as 'disabled'. I refer to myself and others like me as 'a person with a disability'. I am first and foremost a person. My disability is secondary. And to be honest with you, my disability is not the most interesting thing about me. It's just a physical characteristic such as hair color or eye color."

Many of the rangers were grateful to learn about People First Language that they could now incorporate into the programs they would be giving back at their own parks. The next segment focused on the myths and stereotypes about people with disabilities—myths they all grew up with and stereotypes that were constantly being portrayed on television and in the movies.

"I don't know about you, but the movies I saw when I was growing up portrayed people with disabilities as either pitiful and helpless, or the 'angry cripple' who was mad at the world for their disability, or overly sweet and childlike. These characterizations of people with disabilities do an enormous disservice to all of us, because they are unrealistic. The fact is that people with disabilities are like everyone else. Some of us are nice, and some of us are jerks, just like everybody else.

"In the end, it's important to remember that disability is not a bad thing or a good thing. It's just a thing."

The second half of the training was hands-on. All the rangers were required to adopt a disability and go out in pairs to try and experience the park as a visitor. They did tasks from wheelchairs or with their eyes covered to simulate blindness. Some had earplugs to simulate being **deaf**. This way they could experience firsthand some of the challenges people experienced at the park. Her unique approach opened minds in a way that words alone couldn't.

It also caught the attention of the park's superintendent, Richard Marks, a tall, striking man who looked a little imposing in uniform. A park superintendent is the same as the mayor of a town and he made a point of coming to Albright Training Center to meet the person responsible for forty "disabled" rangers struggling to make their way around the hotels and exhibits.

Eileen and Karen considered it a good sign that Superintendent Marks had come to meet her. Eileen found him to be forward-thinking and eager to learn more about how to improve accessibility.

After chatting for about half an hour, he looked at her and said, "This park and other parks have some work to do to become more accessible. If I thought I could find someone to do this full time, I'd hire them tomorrow."

"I'll do it," Eileen heard herself say as casually as if she were accepting a glass of water. She felt it in her bones; she needed to act.

There it is. The opportunity Josef and I predicted.

Later that day she finally rode one of the mules. She rode with Ron Clayton, the head wrangler in charge of all things mule related, and the assistant wrangler. It was a half mile ride on the trail leading into the canyon. Then she turned around and rode back up. The purpose of this ride was to show that someone who has a disability can have the equitation skills to participate on the mule ride.

"It's plain to see that someone with a disability can have adequate skills to ride the mules," said Ron.

Mission accomplished.

Eileen was offered a full-day ride down into the canyon, but it would have extended her trip by several days. While she knew

Zanadu was in good hands, she was anxious to get back to her. Eileen did appreciate the offer, as well as the opportunity to demonstrate her riding skills. More importantly, she found satisfaction in opening their eyes to a world of possibilities.

Eileen didn't know it yet, but she was on the verge of making history at Grand Canyon National Park.

CHAPTER 17

The following spring, Eileen would start her job as a park ranger. Unbeknownst to her, Karen had something brewing back at the canyon. Her friendship with Karen had grown over the past months, and Eileen knew she had a strong **ally** in the woman who would soon become her boss. One evening, shortly before Eileen was scheduled to leave, she got a call.

"Hello, it's Karen. I have some incredible news to share!"

Eileen thought she could hear a smile in her voice.

"Oh? I'd love to hear it," said Eileen.

"As you know, one of the physical requirements of interpretive rangers is to hike to the bottom of the canyon at least once a year to give rangers first-hand knowledge of the terrain. Since it isn't possible to go down in a wheelchair, a few of us have been urging park management to consider allowing you to use your personal horse to help you perform your duties."

"It's the perfect solution! Thank you for suggesting it!"

"I support this plan a hundred percent, but I can't take credit for the idea," said Karen. "Scott Berkenfield brought it up during a meeting. He's a law enforcement ranger assigned to horse patrol because of his extensive horse experience. Someone asked how you were going to get around the canyon since seventy to eighty percent of the job is as a naturalist ranger. Scott said, 'Well if she has specialized horses, why doesn't she bring one?'"

"I love it! What can I do to help?" asked Eileen.

"I can't promise you this will happen. It's a big ask. Park regulations prohibit personal horses; only government horses are allowed. So, there are hoops we still need to jump through."

Eileen was okay with hoops; it was the walls that proved most challenging.

"Has the park service ever approved something like this before?" asked Eileen.

"Never!" Karen answered emphatically. "This type of arrangement hasn't been attempted at any national park. This will be a first. And if management agrees, there are some stipulations."

"Of course. What are they?"

"Part of the agreement is that your horse can't cost the park a penny or man-hours. You'll be completely responsible for the feeding and care."

"That's fair," said Eileen.

"Even though the closest feed store is in Flagstaff, about an hour and a half away?"

"I'll make it work." Eileen preferred caring for her horse anyway.

"And there's still the matter of the evaluation. It will be conducted by Scott."

"I have every confidence in Guenivere. We'll do fine."

"I'm sure you will, but on the off chance you don't, you'd be responsible for shipping her back to Santa Cruz."

"Understood," said Eileen with a nod. "What are my chances?" A twinge of concern crept in knowing that this would require some open-minded thinking from the NPS.

"I won't sugar coat it. There are some people in management that aren't in favor of the idea, but Scott's support carries a lot of weight. I felt good enough about it to pick up the phone and let you know it's a definite maybe."

"I'll take it." Eileen smiled, feeling overjoyed. "Thank you from the bottom of my heart. I know this wouldn't even be under consideration if you and Scott didn't understand that Guenivere isn't a pet or a recreational outlet for me. She's my partner, and I'm grateful that you both recognize how she can be a substitute for a wheelchair."

Scott and Karen understood that her horse was a physical **accommodation** that would enable her to gain the knowledge she needed as an interpretive ranger. From Guenivere's back, Eileen could experience the trails like her fellow rangers.

"Well, it's the right thing to do," said Karen.

When Eileen hung up the phone, she thought, *Hooray for Karen for being a strong advocate and ally of the disability community, and hooray for Scott for seeing possibilities where others saw only obstacles.*

The idea of bringing Guenivere had crossed her mind before, but Eileen hadn't voiced her thoughts to anyone at the canyon yet. Guenivere's training at Dragon Slayers and her willingness to do whatever Eileen asked of her made her the best partner for a rider with a disability hoping to blaze some new trails at Grand Canyon National Park.

In May of 1982, Eileen loaded up her little blue pickup and hit the road, heading to the Grand Canyon yet again. This time she would be starting her new job as park ranger. As a National Park Service interpretive ranger, she would be responsible for educating visitors about the history of the area and teaching about its geology, wildlife, and vegetation. She was offered a nine-month position at the Yavapai Museum of Geology with the option of returning the following season.

The museum was located at Yavapai Point, the second lookout after entering Grand Canyon National Park. It's one of the most photographed locations as both the canyon and the river are visible from this spot. The museum was designed by geologists and built at the edge of the rim with Kaibab limestone sourced from the area. The dramatic, sweeping view of the canyon can be seen from inside the museum.

Excitement bubbled in her chest for the adventure ahead, but it wasn't easy to leave behind all that was familiar and loved. Her friends, family, the redwoods, and the ocean, would soon be exchanged for new friends, co-workers, canyon visitors, cacti, and the desert. Her friend Pam would be especially hard to leave, though she knew she had her full support. It was Pam, after all, who had introduced her to Grand Canyon National Park.

Leaving Josef and the magical kingdom of the Dragon Slayers stung the most. That's where she had learned the greatest life lessons to date. For the first time in her life, she had an invaluable sense of belonging and, at long last, a sense of disability pride.

A lump formed in her throat as she thought about her mentor, her Merlin, who believed in her before she even believed in herself. The wind whipped her hair this way and that as she headed east on Interstate 40. The rushing wind made her think of cantering up the hill toward Josef. She could almost see him standing there on the side of the road, encouraging her to tackle this next adventure. And the most peculiar thing happened. The farther she drove, the less she was thinking about what she was leaving behind. Eileen smiled, unfurled her wings, and let her heart soar.

There comes a time when every apprentice must leave their master and set out for places unknown. While she had left the magic and security of the Dragon Slayer ranch, this was the moment the quest for Camelot began. There would be dragons, even in the desert—the twin dragons of fear and doubt. It would be more important than ever to recall the wisdom Josef had shared with her.

Eileen reported to Karen's office when she arrived.

"Here's the paperwork you need to fill out for hiring and assignment of living quarters," said Karen, who was now officially her supervisor.

Eileen dug in her bag for her blue felt pen. She wasn't a fan of ballpoints. They were difficult for her to write with. She smiled and tucked into the pile of paperwork.

"All done!" said Eileen while handing Karen the packet of papers.

"Great! Let's go sort out your badge and uniform."

Later in Karen's office, Eileen inspected her crisp, new, government-issued shirt, pants, and hat. They had recently changed the style; men and women wore the same uniform now. She'd get another set for the fall and winter months.

The Park Service didn't tailor the uniform for her. Eileen was unable to fasten the buttons on her shirt and pants. She certainly couldn't thread a needle. Zippers were tricky too, but she had a solution: she threaded a string through the zipper tug to create a loop that she could pull.

Eileen sighed louder than she intended.

"Need help with something?" asked Patricia, a fellow ranger.

"Maybe." Eileen smiled sheepishly. "These buttons aren't going to work for me. I have permission to make adaptations to my uniform if the changes aren't visible, but I can't sew. Is there a seamstress in the village?"

"Not that I know of, but I don't have any plans this evening. I can help."

"That would be wonderful! Thank you."

The rest of the day was spent training to be an interpretive ranger. She would train with Karen the next day too. Eileen was hired too late in the season to participate in the seasonal ranger training program, but the biology, geology, and natural history courses she took in college proved most useful while interpreting natural resources.

Eileen settled into her new living quarters at the end of the day. It was a sparsely furnished efficiency apartment, separate from the other rangers. It was the only accessible place, but Eileen didn't mind the location.

By sundown on Eileen's first day, she knew she could do it. She would bring Guenivere to the canyon. She saw firsthand that the space would work for her and her horse. Even though Guenivere was only conditionally approved, Eileen was confident they would do great, and it was well worth the risk. But getting her horse from Santa Cruz to the Grand Canyon would take some coordinating, a weekend off, and a good friend who enjoyed adventures as much as she did.

CHAPTER 18

The next day, she donned the uniform for the first time. She smiled at the young woman in the mirror. The cotton blend shirt and the pants had a nice feel to them, and the uniform fit her perfectly. She tilted her head and squinted.

My crutches will certainly make me stand out from the other rangers. But the fit of the pants hide my leg braces. Her eyebrows went up. *I look more like an injured ranger than a ranger with a disability.*

Most people who used crutches on a regular basis used metal crutches that clamp onto the forearms. Hers were wooden because her disability also included her hands and forearms, making the metal crutches unusable for her.

Later in Karen's office, she ran into Patricia. "What do you think about the Stratton?" she asked.

"To be honest, it reminds me of Smokey the Bear. While he looks fantastic wearing it, I can't say I love it on me." Eileen chuckled.

Patricia's smile grew, "It doesn't do a great job with sun protection either, but it sure does make us look official."

Eileen couldn't disagree. But she already decided she'd reserve the hat for official business and picture day if she could get away with it.

Sure enough, on her first day as a ranger, nearly every visitor who encountered her commented on the crutches. Most tried to be funny.

"What did you do, fall in the canyon?" they'd say and chuckle.

Some people weren't funny; they were just insensitive.

"Did they hire you to be the bad example?" said one guy, shaking his head.

Eileen took a deep breath and heard Josef's voice saying, "Turn obstacles into opportunities."

She knew the sight of her didn't fit their image of a park ranger or their stereotype of a person with a disability. They assumed she was on crutches because she had some sort of athletic injury. They'd never seen someone with a disability in a uniform. Eileen decided to make each interaction an opportunity to raise awareness about people with disabilities and their rights.

But at the end of each day, after responding to nearly a hundred comments about her disability, she was exhausted and annoyed by the careless remarks. As she laid in bed waiting for sleep to whisk her away, she replayed some of the comments that were said to her that day and cringed. Eileen didn't mind being asked questions, but what frustrated her were the invasive and inappropriate ones.

"Can you have children?" one man asked.

She looked him right in the eye and said with a smile, "Is that a marriage proposal?"

These were the only comments she wanted to reply with: "It's none of your business." She reminded herself that she was only one of a handful of people with disabilities in uniform.

My attitude and response will shape the way they interact with other people with disabilities. The only thing any of us have control over is how we respond to a situation. So, what now?

The next morning Eileen, dressed in uniform, leaned against the short wall protecting her from the steep descent of the canyon. Her eyes swept over the magnificent, pastel layers that looked more like a painting than her reality. She took one last cleansing breath before turning her eyes to the crowd. Visitors were still trickling in for her first presentation of the day. She exhaled the inevitable stress that accompanied the unwelcome comments she knew were sitting on the tips of at least half of the tongues in front of her. But today would be different. She had a plan.

Her introduction began basically like all the ranger's intros, "Welcome to Grand Canyon National Park. My name is Eileen Szychowski, and I'm from Santa Cruz, California. Before we begin our geology talk, I'd like to put your minds at ease about why you're seeing a ranger on crutches."

Adding the twist that would set the tone for the rest of her presentation, she stated, "I'm not an injured ranger. I'm a ranger with a disability."

And because she knew that virtually everyone who heard the word "disability" thought of it as bad news, she followed up with,

"And that's not bad news; that's *good* news, because it means that people with disabilities can have a career as a National Park Service Ranger like anyone else."

This tactic diverted a lot of comments, but not all. Thankfully, she had a gift for words and patience. Patience was her superpower. If it was a tangible thing, it would stretch the length of the Colorado River. Eileen stayed levelheaded and responded with humor whenever possible.

One of the many times she was asked if she had fallen in the canyon, the conversation took an unexpected turn.

Eileen took in the woman's appearance. She was tall and thin, with a sophisticated countenance about her. But she wore a T-shirt with "I heart Hanoverians" printed on it, a horse breed often used for jumping and dressage. Eileen told the woman that she did not fall in the canyon, but that she was a ranger with a disability.

The woman's face flushed. Her shoulders curled like she might be considering a nice den to hide herself in. Rescuing the woman from her embarrassment, Eileen said, "I like your shirt."

"Oh!" Her eyes lit up. "Are you familiar with Hanoverians?"

"I am," said Eileen. "I'm a horsewoman too."

The woman introduced herself as Tina and what started as an awkward conversation sparked a lifelong friendship.

Eileen's well of strength was forged through life experiences but fortified by her allies. She was grateful for her fellow rangers. She found their support and encouragement uplifting. One of her fellow rangers used a people counter to track how many times visitors made cracks about her use of crutches or commented on her disability, and, on an average day, it was in the nineties.

Josef's teachings lived in the back of her mind and the center of her heart. They were a constant comfort. But Eileen was also gifted with tools of her own that proved invaluable. Words are powerful things. They're invisible yet bursting with their own sort of magic that can win wars, build castles, or, conversely, destroy confidence and cause harm. Eileen learned to wield her words like a sword and did her best to take control of situations with well-chosen phrases. She didn't hide from what was uncomfortable; she faced it head-on with Excalibur gleaming.

CHAPTER 19

Eileen originally planned to bring one horse to the canyon, but as fate would have it, she would end up with two horses and a goose. She requested that she bring her Arabian horse, Janik, along as a companion for Guenivere. The two park horses were going to be taken over to the North Rim for a few weeks before being sent to pasture for the winter. Park management understood it wouldn't be good for Guenivere to be alone, and since Janik wouldn't be used on the job, it wasn't a problem.

But the goose was another story.

Eileen laid her map on the table.

"It's a two day drive each way," she mumbled to herself. "I'll need a horse-friendly place to camp. I'll rent a U-Haul truck and horse trailer at home. I still need to book a flight to Santa Cruz. Easy."

She reached out to her old friend Mark to see if he could help transport the horses. As a teacher, he had summers off and was always up for an adventure. She would also need his help driving the truck and trailer since the rental didn't have the necessary **adaptive equipment** Eileen required to operate it.

Mark said yes. His only request was that he could bring his motorcycle. He wanted to spend an extra day or two exploring Northern Arizona and the Sedona area before returning the truck and trailer to the U-Haul place in Flagstaff. He'd then ride his motorcycle home.

Eileen was grateful for the company and the security of traveling with a good friend. Plus, it's no small undertaking traveling with horses. If anything happened on the trip, she would need an extra set of hands. The next available weekend, she was back home and getting ready for another road trip.

Mark met Eileen at the U-Haul center to pick up the truck and horse trailer, then headed to Dragon Slayers to pick up the horses. When they pulled up the drive to Josef's ranch, Eileen spotted Zanadu happily floating in a tub of water, surrounded by a fence. Zanadu's overnight bag was packed.

Eileen furrowed her eyebrows in confusion, "What's this? Joanne is supposed to keep her while I'm away."

Josef smiled, "Sweetie, you just have to take her with you. Everything will be better if you do."

"I don't think bringing a goose to the park is allowed," she protested.

"I just have a feeling that you and all your animals need to stay together," he said.

There was no arguing with Josef. They packed the four bales of hay in the back of the U-Haul, in between the motorcycle and the goose nursery. They loaded the horses, said their farewells, then took off toward Grand Canyon.

The first day they took a lunch break in Needles, California at a rest stop for campers and RVs on the edge of the Colorado River at the border between Arizona and California. They let the horses out of the trailer to stretch their legs and cool off.

"I bet Zanadu would love to swim in the river," said Mark.

"I assure you she does not," said Eileen.

"She's a goose! It's hot. She'll love it."

"She won't." Eileen shook her head. "Geese don't like fast-moving currents like this."

"Oh, come on, I'll tie a rope around her leg so she can't go far."

The corner of Eileen's lips raised in an amused grin. She shrugged. "It's your funeral."

"She can't weigh more than eleven pounds. What could happen?" said Mark confidently.

He waded in the water with Zanadu in his arms, her makeshift safety tether attached. It was a comical sight to see a six-foot-four man with a goose going for a dip together in the river. He sunk down a little deeper in the water, and Zanadu felt the current and panicked, just as Eileen had predicted. Her long wings flapped in Mark's face as she struggled to get to shallow water and back to the shore. His height was probably the only thing that kept him from going under as he wrestled the frantic goose.

Both Mark and Zanadu made it out safely, but it was a grand I-told-you-so moment for Eileen. Zanadu was ecstatic to be back in her tub.

Back on the road, their truck started losing power while crossing the Mohave Desert. That was tricky because they had to find a service station that was approved to service U-Haul vehicles. Eileen got a kick out of the mechanic's expression when Mark opened the back of the truck and revealed the goose floating in a tub of water next to the bales of hay.

"My wife is never going to believe this," he said.

They got the truck fixed and camped a few hours down the road in an empty fairground outside of Kingman, Arizona. It was a good spot because they were able to turn the horses out overnight.

The next day they arrived at Grand Canyon without further incident. Eileen could never have gotten her horses to Grand Canyon without the help of this good friend. She never forgot Mark's kindness.

Turns out Zanadu was the first and only domestic goose to ever witness a sunset at the Grand Canyon. Knowing this made the official letter for breaking park regulations worth it. Karen, however, loved Zanadu and thought it was great that Eileen brought her along. Eileen placed credit for this mischievous mission to Josef, but it turns out Zanadu did have an important role to play.

In Santa Cruz, Eileen had taken Zanadu to Mark's classroom. He left the Skills Center before her and was teaching at the Alternative School, a program for teens who learned better in a non-traditional classroom setting. Zanadu was a beautiful, feathered metaphor to encourage the kids not to give up. Eileen wanted to visit classrooms with her at Grand Canyon too. Zanadu was the original Visiting Critter in a program Eileen would start one day in the future. It would be a program aimed at educating kids in public schools about disability issues. With an enchanted goose as her sidekick, Eileen could always count on having the kids' attention.

Eileen and Zanadu sat together listening to the munching sounds of Guenivere and Janik while watching the show before them unfold. The golden sun sank slowly in the sky, leaving brilliant hues of orange, pink, purple, and blue in its wake. The stars awoke, twinkling their hellos, and Eileen felt content. If she were a goose, she'd hum.

Even though Josef had to convince her that it would be better to have all three critters together in one place, she had to admit he was right. She had faith in him and that it would all work out as it should.

CHAPTER 20

The aim of the evaluation was to assess her horsemanship skills as well as her horse's ability to handle crowds, rocky terrain, busy road traffic, and unexpected activity by rowdy campers. She would be given no special consideration. With so much at stake, Eileen and her horse would be held to the same rigorous standards as every other park ranger and park horse.

Scott met her at the barn. He would be riding Sierra, the big, black Quarter Horse gelding ridden by the law enforcement rangers. Eileen, of course, was on Guenivere. Eyes turned their direction as they rode through the park on their striking horses, and many people stopped to take photos. Even the visitors on the tour buses pointed and snapped pictures. Camera phones hadn't been invented yet. Film and development were costly, so it was quite an honor to be photographed.

Each time she heard a camera click, she smiled inwardly, knowing the last thing that would ever cross the photographer's mind was the fact that one of the rangers on horseback wore leg braces and had little use of her hands.

Scott and Eileen chatted as he took her and Guenivere through busy traffic intersections, moving crowds of visitors laden with backpacks and camera equipment, and long lines of tour buses with loud air brakes. Through it all, Guenivere maintained her calm demeanor, even as they rode through the tourist-packed plaza of the Bright Angel Lodge, where dozens of visitors asked them to pose for photographs against the backdrop of the canyon.

Leaving the hotels and restaurants behind, they rode along the Rim Trail. After a bit, they veered off into a wooded area, eventually arriving at an outdoor amphitheater. An interpretive ranger was leading a Junior Ranger program for about a dozen kids. The amphitheater contained a semicircle of long wooden benches carved from large logs, all facing an outdoor stage made of concrete. They emerged from the woods and were spotted by the youngsters, who were so excited that the ranger leading the program invited Eileen and Scott to stay and answer questions about their horses.

Guenivere had done well with everything Scott had thrown at them, but now he had one more challenge to test their abilities.

"Do you think your horse would go up the concrete stairs leading onto the stage?" he asked.

Eileen had confidence in Guenivere and said, "Yes, I think so."

Scott's horse was hesitant, so he moved aside for Eileen and Guenivere. Up the stairs and onto the stage they went—clop, clop, clop—with Scott's horse following close behind.

Here she was, seated on a horse in the uniform of a park ranger, looking down at all the admiring young faces from atop a stage.

She couldn't help but ask herself, "How many girls with disabilities are doing this today?" The answer that immediately came to mind was, "Not enough, but someday there will be others."

The next day, Karen informed her that Scott's report was very positive. They had passed with flying colors and a little bit of history was made as she went from being a visitor denied the mule ride based on disability to becoming a ranger on horseback, all in the space of a year.

None of this could've happened without Guenivere. Her dependable nature and her training as a Dragon Slayer horse served her well in her capacity as a ranger's mount, and it would continue to serve her well when she became Camelot's first school horse. Eileen would one day owe this generous horse more than could ever be repaid in a single lifetime.

The thrum of the day finally quieted to a gentle hum. The voices of visitors fizzled away. A smile bloomed from ear to ear as it hit her square in the heart—*she was the first mounted ranger in the National Park Service with a physical disability.*

CHAPTER 21

It wasn't until Eileen had been at Grand Canyon for about a month that she was finally able to see it in all its glory from the back of a horse. Guenivere had been living at sea level in the moist climate of coastal California and needed a few weeks to adapt to the 7,200-foot elevation and extremely dry environment of Arizona's high desert.

To prepare for the two-day ride that would take them down to the bottom of the canyon and back up, they rode a few shorter rides about halfway down the canyon. They also explored trails not normally open to visitors.

Superintendent Marks arranged for Eldon Bowman, a colleague of his who was an experienced horse outfitter, to accompany her on these rides. She was grateful to have an experienced riding partner as the trails were narrow and challenging. Anything could happen at any time, and it would be foolhardy for any rider, disabled or not, to ride in the canyon alone. Eldon proved to be an enjoyable and helpful riding buddy.

After two successful one-day rides into the inner canyon with Eldon, they arranged the overnight trip that would take them all the way down the Bright Angel Trail. They'd stay at the world-famous Phantom Ranch at the bottom of the canyon. The only way to reach the ranch from the South Rim is to cross the Bright Angel Trail Suspension Bridge, a metal bridge spanning 440 feet several stories above the Colorado River.

The trail from the rim to Phantom Ranch was nearly eight miles one-way. Eileen was looking forward to the rib-sticking dinner of cowboy food and the overnight stay in the dormitory-style cabin before tackling the trip back up.

They began the ride in the early morning, which would put them into the shaded areas of the canyon during the hottest part of the afternoon. After several hours of riding down the seemingly endless switchbacks, descending through layers of color and time, they finally reached the bridge. Guenivere had experience traversing metal bridges, which gave Eileen confidence that she would cross it without hesitation despite being able to see through the planks and the sides to the churning Colorado River below.

As Guenivere stepped onto the bridge, Eileen gasped at the breathtaking view of the inner canyon. As they approached the middle of the gently swaying bridge, she had to stop for a few moments to take in the beauty around her and marvel at what it took to get there. Poised several stories above the river, with a soft breeze fluttering through her hair and her horse's mane, she was able to see miles of the inner canyon in both directions. It was an otherworldly experience.

Once at Phantom Ranch, all four of them—Eldon, Eileen, and their two horses—welcomed a good night's sleep and a hearty cowboy breakfast the next morning before heading back up the Bright Angel Trail.

As they were leaving the ranch, Eileen had an idea.

"Eldon, would you mind if we left the trail for a moment to ride to the river's edge?"

"Sure, lead the way," he said.

As they got closer to the river, the dry, sandy beach gave way to moist, firm footing. Her smile was wide when she saw the myriad of animal tracks all leading to and from the river. Eileen recognized the unmistakable tracks of deer, the paw prints of coyote, the prehistoric-looking tracks of a massive bird, most likely a Great Blue Heron, the tiny tracks of a squirrel, and even tinier sets of tracks which were probably from a large lizard or iguana.

Gazing with wonderment at all the footprints, she fully understood that the Colorado River is the beating heart of the Grand Canyon. Every living thing in and around the canyon depended on the river for its daily life. She wanted to get off her horse and be as close to the river as possible.

"Eldon, would you mind helping me dismount, please?"

After assisting her off her horse, he handed Eileen her crutches. She walked across the moist sand to the water's edge. It felt wonderful to touch the river that she'd waited so long to reach.

She spent several minutes watching, listening to, and experiencing the grandeur of the river. Finally, she made her way back to her patiently-waiting horse and, with Eldon's assistance, got back on Guenivere. As they turned their horses to begin their eight-mile uphill trek out of the canyon, something inside her made her look over her shoulder to see where she had been. It was then that Eileen noticed a new pair of tracks: a set of crutch tracks intermingled with those of coyote, deer, lizard, and heron—a sight that made her feel that she was part of it all too. For a moment, she felt just a teensy bit like Neil Armstrong, the first human to leave footprints on the moon.

As satisfying as it was to see crutch prints at the bottom of the canyon, she knew it would be so much more satisfying when such a sight would become commonplace. That would only happen when more people with disabilities were permitted to ride the mules and participate in the river rafting trips like everyone else.

Chapter 22

Eileen laid back in the bed of her little blue pickup truck and stared into the canopy of the tall trees looming above her. They weren't the great redwoods she found at home, but rather the strong pines of Northern Arizona. One of her favorite pastimes was driving into the woods by herself to soak in all nature had to offer. Her eyes closed as she focused on the music from the songbirds.

She turned her head with her eyes still shut. She could swear she heard the ocean. She didn't want to ruin the illusion that the wind weaving through miles of pine needles provided her. They sounded so much like waves. But when the breeze caressed her skin, one crucial ingredient was missing. The wind brought the scent of pine instead of the sea. She couldn't help but wonder if this was a message from Josef. Change in the air.

Eileen was past the growing pains of learning a new job. She was comfortable in her role as an interpretive ranger but enjoyed her other duties as well. Her work with Karen was important. They designed the park's programs and exhibits to be more accessible for people with various disabilities. Eileen smiled thinking about the 3-D models of the canyon they now had on display and the braille that was added to exhibits so that people who are blind or visually impaired could experience it all for themselves.

The disability awareness training for the employees at Grand Canyon was gratifying too. She worked with a lot of different people, not just the rangers. People from the hotels and restaurants came to learn, and even the tour and shuttle bus drivers sat in on her trainings.

*But my favorite thing...*she thought. No, not favorite. It was more than that.

The most important part of my job is demonstrating that the job itself could be done by anyone with a disability who met the qualifications and had the desire to work at a national park.

Her work as a ranger was immensely satisfying, but the day-to-day reality of living at the park was challenging for someone on crutches. The living quarters for the rangers either involved stairs or lots of walking over uneven terrain. The one-room apartment she was assigned to didn't have a laundry room. She had to carry her sack of laundry to and from the communal washer and dryers, all of which became even more challenging once the winter snows came.

At the end of every day, she was exhausted. After feeding her horses at the park service barn near the ranger residential area and visiting Zanadu each evening, she went back to her tiny quarters. She didn't have a television, internet, or even a radio. She fell asleep enjoying a book.

She heard a familiar and welcomed voice carried on a breeze.

"But is it worth it, my dear?"

Josef.

"It is," she said to the wind. "All of this is worth it."

She loved it when there was someone in the audience who had a disability or who had a child or a relative with a disability. How their face would light up when they heard her story. None of this was because she wanted to be in the limelight. In fact, that was the most taxing part of it all for her. It would have been a much easier path to stay away from such a public job. But Eileen's calling at the canyon was to show people what was possible.

It filled her heart when people came up to her after a presentation to tell her how thrilling it was to see someone with a disability working as a ranger. When she mentioned having a horse to help her do her job, parents would often request that she ride to their campground so that their disabled son or daughter could meet her and Guenivere. Eileen smiled at the memory of one such interaction.

She waited until the youngster in the wheelchair asked to pet her horse before telling them that she, too, had a disability.

"You do? Where?" the wide-eyed youngster asked.

"Come closer and look under my pant legs," she invited. "And check out my hands."

"No way!"

A reaction that made her day.

"You know what this means don't you?" Eileen asked. "It means that you, too, can be a park ranger someday if that's something you'd like to do."

I loved doing that! I especially loved knowing that, at first glance, the camper in the wheelchair had no idea that, like them, I wore leg braces and had a hand disability.

That fed her soul. There were moments that made her laugh too, like the time the mechanic who fixed the truck when she and Mark broke down in the Mohave Desert ended up in her tour group.

Afterward, he came up with his wife and asked, "Do you remember me? I fixed your U-Haul a while back."

Eileen nodded. "Yes, of course! You saved us! You helped me get here."

"Could you tell my wife what was in the back of your truck? She doesn't believe me."

That was a fun day!

She was always rewarded with something wonderful. Like an uplifting interaction with a park visitor that reminded her of the end goal. And through it all, there was the never-ending beauty of the canyon to feed her soul.

Eileen's hand crunched the magazine lying next to her as she sat up from the bed of her truck. The wind blew the pages open to an article she had been reading earlier about the Arabian horses in Scottsdale, Arizona. She'd been getting these magazines for years. They touted how Scottsdale was the center of the horse community in Arizona. She had known when she left Santa Cruz for Grand Canyon that she would set up Camelot in the Scottsdale area. Eileen was settled in her new home, even though she knew her time in the canyon was quickly coming to an end. Before long, the journey to Camelot would be upon her.

Yes, change is in the air.

THE QUEENDOM

Her bright clear eyes in sunlight glow'd;
On burnish'd hooves her war-horse trode;
From underneath her helmet flow'd
Her dark-brown hair as on she rode,
As she rode on to Camelot.

~ Adapted from The Lady of Shallot (1832),
Alfred, Lord Tennyson

Chapter 23

Superintendent Marks came to see Eileen on her last day of work as a seasonal ranger. "Thank you for the work that you did. But I know there's still a lot that needs to be done. If you would like to come back next season, the door's still open."

"Thank you, but it's time for me to begin my program. Will you hire another disabled person in my place?" asked Eileen.

"If you find me someone else like you, I will."

"I promise I will find you at least two like me," said Eileen with a smile. She partnered with the disabled student services at Northern Arizona University in Flagstaff and already had a couple of students in mind.

Both Eileen and Superintendent Marks fulfilled their promises.

Eileen attracted lots of media attention from local and national television news. Initially, it was because she was the first mounted ranger at Grand Canyon who had a physical disability. Good Morning America with Erma Bombeck did a special piece on her. Prior to this, all of Erma's pieces were humorous and done in the studio. Her producer was so impressed with the feedback from Eileen's segment that Erma's contract was rewritten to include additional out-of-studio human interest stories. Word got to Eileen that Erma was thrilled with this new opportunity.

CBS and ABC affiliates in Arizona also came to the Canyon to film news segments. Print publications made the trek too, such as the *Arizona Republic* from Phoenix and *The Arizona Daily Sun* from Flagstaff. There was a long list of Associated Press newspapers from across the country that picked up the press release from the National Park Service.

Whether she intended it or not, Eileen was officially a public figure, advocating for people with disabilities. She carried the responsibility proudly but struggled being in the spotlight. During the summer, several visitors from other parts of the country said they'd read about a disabled mounted ranger at Grand Canyon in their local newspaper and had hoped to meet her when they visited. Some even asked if she could strap her crutches to her saddle to "prove that she was disabled" as they took her picture.

She declined. Eileen always left her crutches at the barn when riding in uniform.

"My purpose in serving as a ranger at Grand Canyon is to prove 'ability' not 'disability'. Also, my English saddle doesn't allow for the strapping on of objects," she told them.

Additional TV and magazine coverage continued after she moved to Phoenix. Having a disability always brought her attention, and now, by following her dreams, she would inevitably attract more of it. But this, she knew, would be helpful in the next chapter. She would sing from the hilltops to anyone who would listen. Eileen needed support to build the kind of program she had in mind.

In May of 1982, Eileen told a reporter, "Some people laugh at my plan. Here I have no money, and I'm raising a kingdom in the desert . . . Josef taught me how to dream, and he told me don't dream small."

Eileen kissed Guinevere and Janik on their noses. They were staying with Eldon, the horse outfitter she knew from the canyon. He had a ranch in Flagstaff and boarded them for her. Zanadu was staying with a ranger friend. Eileen looked up at the gray sky as snowflakes landed gently on her face. She smiled. It brought her peace knowing her animals were left in good care while she searched for accommodations.

Unfortunately, the media attention didn't come with a paycheck. She had $100 in her pocket and a lot of faith in her heart as she began the two-and-a-half-hour drive south to the Valley of the Sun, the nickname given to the Phoenix metropolitan area. Before long the gentle December snow turned into a blizzard and her truck slipped off the road. Thankfully, she was rescued by a motorist who stopped to help. Safely on the road again, she continued her journey.

The snow-covered pines of Flagstaff were quickly replaced by saguaro cacti and creosote. She was surrounded by a spectacular, rocky landscape and the gray sky turned blue. While there were some long, straight stretches of road, most of it was dramatic, swooping curves that headed downhill and around the mountains. Two hours later, she was in a T-shirt on the border of Phoenix.

"Okay," she said to herself after about thirty more minutes of driving, "Where are the green fields filled with horses that I saw in the magazines?"

Her heart sunk. It didn't take her long to learn that the pastures she fell in love with were rare and located in the most exclusive area of the Valley. They were well outside her budget.

This wasn't the beginning she was hoping for. She didn't even know where she was going to spend her first night.

Maybe I'll stay at the Arabian horse show grounds.

Eileen decided to take a chance on a woman she met while presenting at a two-day workshop at the park called Winners Against the Odds. It was for educators and service providers. Eileen was the keynote speaker teaching about building opportunities for adults with disabilities, employment, and independent living. Vicki was one of the attendees and said if she ever needed a place to stay while in Phoenix to give her a call.

Eileen now recognized when the Universe set the right people in her path and decided to take Vicki up on the offer. They were acquaintances at best, essentially strangers, yet Vicki was so accommodating. Eileen was worried about Zanadu, but she, too, was welcomed with open arms. They stayed with Vicki for a few weeks, giving Eileen time to get settled.

There had been another attendee at the conference who introduced herself during the break. Lauren DeVuyst was a professional woman who also lived and worked in Phoenix. She was an experienced horsewoman and would become Camelot's first volunteer. After meeting these generous strangers, Eileen became more and more convinced that this was the right place to establish Camelot.

Eileen quickly found horse country and a barn with stall space she could afford. She set up shop at Santa Rita Stables in Phoenix, which was located west of Scottsdale and nearly 730 miles from Santa Cruz, California. It wasn't what she expected, but things rarely are.

Eileen didn't want to lose the momentum, and, within the first week, she met with a lawyer to get Camelot's incorporation paperwork underway. She set up speaking engagements with numerous service groups and disability organizations, acquiring new volunteers and new students along the way.

By mid-February 1983, less than ninety days after moving to the Valley, Camelot was officially founded. Guenivere traded in the green fleece saddle pad of the ranger's mount for the white saddle pad of Camelot's first school horse. It all began with her and soon other exceptional horses, hand-picked by Eileen, would join the ranks of the first therapeutic riding program to be established in Arizona.

CHAPTER 24

Eileen never forgot what it was like to tuck her dreams away in a box, or the feeling of prying open the lid and letting them gallop free. She was gifted with the opportunity and grand responsibility to help others do the same. She shared the personal victories of her students with Josef through letters and the articles she mailed to him.

"This is the greatest reward I could ever hope for," he wrote back.

Horse dreams come in all shapes and sizes, but there were a few things every Camelot rider had in common. They shared a love of horses. Her students were there because they wanted to be, not just because someone else wanted it for them. And they had a disability. Often, kids wanted to experience an outdoor activity like their non-disabled peers. Horses and horsemanship gave them that something extra to feel good about and it was a great conversation starter at school.

Many of the students were born with their disabilities and just as many were not. Some students' disabilities were the result of an accident or serious illness such as meningitis, polio, or cancer.

"Trevor" was one such young rider whose disabilities were the result of a nearly lifelong battle with childhood cancer and its aftermath. At age ten, he'd already faced more challenges than most people face in a lifetime of eighty years or more. His cancer had spread, and his parents understood that he would not likely make it to his eleventh birthday. Knowing this, his mom sought out activities that would bring him joy. His dream was to be a cowboy. Despite the risk involved for a child requiring portable oxygen and an ostomy bag, Trevor's mom saw to it that he was able to be a regular kid at a stable.

Thanks to a great team of volunteers and a kind gelding named Vivo, who didn't give a second thought to having a portable oxygen tank and several feet of tubing strapped to the saddle, Trevor was able to ride off into the sunset as a real Arizona cowboy.

Jim, a forty-something polio survivor, had been using a wheelchair since contracting the disease at age nineteen. He came to Camelot with a very specific horse dream. During the week, he was a professional accountant, but outside of work, Jim was a passionate Civil War buff who had been participating for several years in large-scale reenactments of various battles. He was frustrated that, due to his wheelchair, he was always assigned one of the less exciting, earthbound jobs such as that of quartermaster. His dream was to participate as a member of a mounted unit, so he came to Camelot to learn about horses and horse equipment.

Pursuing his dream would test his abilities to the max; he would need to develop sufficient strength and balance to be able to sit on a horse for an hour or more and ride with enough control to be part of a mounted unit. He planned to retrofit a genuine McClellan Army saddle, the type used by U.S. Army Cavalry during the Civil War, to meet his specific needs. Jim also needed to develop a mounting technique that would work in the field with the help of a good riding buddy.

Lynn Wright, a Camelot volunteer, filled that role, along with a few others. They worked together to figure out the body mechanics and logistics so Jim could get on and off his horse safely on the field. Once these details were hashed out, Jim was able to train his reenactment buddy on how to help. About a year or so later, Jim had developed enough skill and endurance to participate in a major battle reenactment back East.

It was exciting for all the volunteers and students to see the photographs of Jim in a Cavalry uniform, on horseback, indistinguishable from the other soldiers in his unit. Not only did Jim fulfill his dream, but he also carried the message of Camelot into a whole new realm.

But there was one student whose passion for horses and sense of daring took her squarely into the horse community where she would open eyes and challenge perceptions like no other. Like Eileen, Denise Thompson came into the world as a horse lover, despite having no horse people in her family. Like every other horse crazy little girl, she immersed herself in horse stories and watched all the old TV Westerns. Even though she was blind, Denise envisioned having a horse of her own one day.

In early 1983, Eileen gave a presentation at Arizona Bridge to Independent Living (ABIL), where Denise was working. She wasted no time coming up to Eileen afterward to sign up for lessons. She became one of Camelot's first students. Given her educational background and professional skills, Eileen sought her out as a member of the curriculum development committee. This was only the beginning of Denise's commitment to giving back to Camelot.

She took to the lessons like a goose to water. She arrived early and stayed late, as Eileen did at Dragon Slayers. As with other blind or visually impaired students, transportation was an enormous challenge, but even this would not deter her. After about a year, Denise made the decision to purchase a horse of her own. Her breed of choice was a Missouri Fox Trotter, a smooth-gaited horse with a calm disposition. She continued her involvement with Camelot, volunteering and assisting with other students. She took the notion of paying things forward very seriously. Denise joined the Missouri Fox Trotter Association and began to participate on weekend trail rides with members of the club. They had never been around a blind person, let alone a blind horse owner. Each time she participated in an event and each time she went by herself to buy horse equipment at the tack store, the horse world changed a little bit.

After boarding her horse for a while at a local rental stable, struggling with the never-ending obstacles that exist for a blind horse owner, Denise made the decision to buy her own horse property. From there she became a breeder of Missouri Fox Trotters and, eventually, miniature horses. Although these activities kept her busy, she always found time to serve Camelot in some capacity. Her greatest contribution to the program came when she was invited to be on the board of directors, ultimately being named chairperson.

From her start as one of Camelot's earliest students, to serving on its board of directors many years later, Denise would bring the Dragon Slayer philosophy full circle.

Watching Denise fulfill her horse dreams brought Eileen as much, if not more, joy and satisfaction than being able to fulfill her own. As always, Josef was right: the best way to keep a magical thing is to give it away.

CHAPTER 25

Josef's final words to Eileen before she entered the vehicle to leave Santa Cruz for good were some of the most generous and liberating words a mentor could ever utter to a protégé about to begin her own journey.

"Go out and do it your way, my dear. You owe me nothing. Whatever you've learned here, take it, and create a program that feels right to you."

Even early on, she had some definite ideas, one of which was to have a riding program based on a structured curriculum that would blend horsemanship, outdoor education, and independent living skills. The curriculum would be a hybrid and would require a team of individuals with experience and talents in all these areas to help in its development.

Along with Eileen, the committee included Lauren, Denise, Gail Curran, and Shirley Lowman. It was guided by Eileen's friend and colleague Pam Ludwig, who had experience in curriculum development. They met as a team, working in half-day sessions. After many months, they had a dynamic, comprehensive curriculum that could accommodate both children and adults with differing abilities. The curriculum was comprised of three sections: Horses & Horsemanship, Our Place in Nature, and Community Participation.

Using the curriculum as a lesson planning tool, students developed skills and knowledge that went well beyond horsemanship, such as increased confidence and independence at home, at school, and in the community. The curriculum was unique among therapeutic horsemanship programs, most of which focus only on therapeutic goals. The aim was to serve the total person, encouraging independence and active participation in the community. It has survived the test of time and continues to serve as a lesson planning guide for Camelot instructors and volunteers today.

Eileen had a handful of students and volunteers and was fundraising to sustain the program. One of her biggest challenges was when people heard that she offered her services for free, they couldn't see it working as a business model. But she had Dragon Slayers as proof that this could work. And as people listened to her speak, they heard something they hadn't heard before. It touched something in their hearts, and they wanted to be a part of it.

She focused on building the program alongside her growing team of volunteers and supporters. Running Camelot out of rented quarters wasn't ideal, but it worked. Even in this barn that wasn't their forever home, she felt the familiar spark of horse magic as her students, both young and old, lived out their dreams.

Five years after arriving in Phoenix, and with a polished curriculum in place, Eileen knew it was time to search for Camelot's permanent home. While some plans were made with the counsel of her faithful knights, this was an executive decision. It was all hers. In 1989, she wrote a list.

CAMELOT'S HOME WILL BE . . .

~ Located in North Scottsdale, within 20 minutes of present location
~ At least ten acres with safe access to state land
~ Horse permits obtainable, can conduct program activities on site
~ Utilities obtainable at reasonable cost
~ Must lend itself to barrier-free design for wheelchair and crutch users
~ Adjacent to other ranches for emergency type support
~ Safe and secure with low traffic
~ Abundant vegetation, a few washes, mountain vistas
~ Must have a serene feeling where healing, learning, and growing can take place

She included a map of the area she'd consider and this quote: "It is only by risking . . . from one hour to another that we live at all. And often enough, our faith beforehand in an uncertain result is the only thing that makes the result come true." – C. James
Eileen had faith.

The Universe placed another person in her path: Hamilton Wright, Jr. Ham, as his friends called him, was a highly regarded businessman with a lot of connections in the philanthropic community. He had served as a development director for a large hospital and knew how to make nonprofits thrive. Eileen had been introduced to him sometime earlier by one of her volunteers.

She had a feeling she had to ask him for help in developing a capital campaign to fund Camelot's permanent home, so she invited him out to lunch. She didn't know him well but knew him well enough. He was an honorable man with strong ethics and a deep sense of the important things in life. Eileen was convinced he was the mentor she needed for this next phase of the journey.

She talked to him about her dreams for Camelot and said, "I want to know if you will help me raise the kind of money needed to build Camelot a permanent home. I know this is a big thing I'm asking. You don't have to answer me now, but please sleep on it."

He was quiet for a moment and said, "Yes. I'm going to do it. But I'm not doing it for you, Eileen. I'm doing it for Camelot."

While she was a little surprised by his answer, she couldn't have hoped for a better one. This wasn't for her; it was for the program. His answer made it clear that he believed in the work of Camelot.

Later, in one of their planning sessions, Ham said, "The key to fundraising is to be yourself, make it personal, and tell a story."

This advice served her well when he brought her to the attention of some of the major philanthropists in the Valley. Ham was the best person she could have turned to for the guidance and support she needed to make Camelot's permanent home a reality. His personal belief in the program and his standing in the community gave major donors the confidence they needed to invest in a small program. Ham was the knight in shining armor who helped make the capital campaign a success.

Eileen and the Camelot volunteers hosted fundraising events. She continued to speak to service groups and network in the community. Her goal was to purchase land outright and build the "castle" and stables without getting a loan so she could uphold her promise to Josef of not charging for lessons.

In 1990, the ADA was signed, guaranteeing the civil rights for people with disabilities. It was a game changer. It guaranteed that people with disabilities would have the same opportunities as everyone else. They would no longer be held separate; they had the legal right to participate in the mainstream of American life. The act was modeled after the Civil Rights Act of 1964 and prohibits discrimination.

By 1992, they had raised $300,000 to purchase land and Eileen immediately started searching. Camelot urgently needed a home. Donors and sponsors were eager to see their generous contributions used in a timely manner.

There were a lot of properties on the market in the North Scottsdale area at the time, and, after looking at a dozen or so, Eileen realized it was going to take a lot of her time and energy. Since she was tied up during the week giving lessons and running the program, she asked for help from Lynn and another volunteer, Jim, both of whom had owned horse property and knew what she was looking for.

In addition to her original list, there were two major factors driving her decision in the selection of property. Many of the students relied on public transportation to get to their lessons, and since options were limited at the time, the property could not be too far outside the city limits. On the other hand, since Scottsdale was experiencing a development boom, it had to be far enough away from the densely populated areas to avoid encroachment and to allow access to open desert areas for trail riding. In other words, not too far away from town, but not too close either.

Eileen gave them a list of six or seven properties, along with the wish list. She tasked them with selecting the top three, which she would later go and view herself. After a few months, and nearly twenty properties toured, one of those top three candidates was a winner!

A 14.5-acre parcel was available in an undeveloped area that checked all the boxes on the wish list. It was on the market for $35,000 per acre. Eileen made an all-cash offer of $17,500 per acre, half the asking price. The offer was immediately accepted. It was the right place, at the right time, for the right amount of money.

It had taken five years to raise the money to buy the land and would take another five years to raise funding to construct the facility. It also took everyone who sat at The Round Table, believing in a common vision, to bring this dream to fruition.

Eileen's experience as a riding instructor who had a disability, giving lessons at a commercial boarding and training stable, provided her with the insight and problem-solving experience needed for the design of a barrier-free stable. She was also fortunate to have two valuable gentlemen volunteering their building and planning expertise: Lynn, who had also helped her find the property, and Jack Strickstein. They offered continual support and guidance in the design and construction process from start to finish.

They were the best kind of unpaid knights a young woman could have. They made certain that every contractor they met with understood that it was the short gal on crutches making the decisions and signing the checks. To be able to support and empower a person at the same time is the very definition of a knight in shining armor.

It's always easier to make a building accessible from the ground up as opposed to retrofitting an existing building, which can be expensive and sometimes impossible. The biggest requirement for accessibility is having the space to accommodate people using wheelchairs, crutches, and walkers. It was also important to keep blind students in mind in the design of the barn and classroom areas. After much thought and having adult students look over the plans and give input, construction began on their dream facility.

The result was a one-of-a-kind, barrier-free ranch, complete with a tack room, feed room, wash rack, schoolroom, and offices. There's a large arena for lessons, a round pen for training, and trails leading around and through the property.

It's a place where people of all abilities can independently and safely work with and care for horses. The Camelot facility is like no other riding stable or therapeutic horsemanship facility. Someday, hopefully, there will be others.

In 1997, after a sixteen-year journey from Grand Canyon to this moment, the horses, the enchanted goose, and Eileen moved into the castle. Camelot was finally home. Eileen's students would indeed experience the freedom of an accessible ranch, the power that sparked after defeating their personal dragons, and the magic of horses. Just like she had as a student of Dragon Slayers. At the barrier-free ranch, Eileen and her students became masters of their environment. Everyone, regardless of their physical limitations, was able to independently take care of their horses.

Like the redwood tree, Camelot grew slowly, never taking on debt and never accepting more students or horses than the program could handle. Eileen knew that to keep her promise to Josef, owning the property was only part of the equation. She needed to manage Camelot's finances in the long term and be smart with the donations made to the program. She didn't want to waste a single penny on interest for bank loans.

She kept her promise. No student has ever been charged to ride at Camelot.

Each day the barn was filled with the happy sounds of students, volunteers, and staff working side-by-side, learning about and caring for horses. Everyone who came to Camelot realized they were part of something special: The Round Table, wherein each person was both student and teacher. The joy Eileen experienced every time she watched a student advance to the next level reminded her that the place she had been seeking had been seeking her.

At the end of each day's lessons, Eileen watched the last student's car drive through the gate, feeling a sense of gratitude and deep satisfaction at being able to give to others what was given to her by Josef so many years ago. And as she listened to the Camelot horses contentedly munching their dinner in their cozy stalls, she would occasionally ask herself, *How many girls with disabilities are doing this today?* And the answer that always came to her was, *Not enough, but someday there will be others. . .*

EPILOGUE

Camelot was the first therapeutic riding center in Arizona, and to date, it's the longest-running program of its kind in the state. It became the shining star it was destined to be and a point of pride in the Scottsdale community.

Over the course of time, the area surrounding the ranch would indeed become more developed. However, the amount of acreage purchased continues to provide a buffer. It's still a Sonoran Desert retreat from civilization. Owning the land free and clear assures that Camelot's home will be secure for generations to come. Today, the Camelot property is worth millions. Though, the people who come through the gate might argue it's worth even more.

No one ever likes to say goodbye, but alas, to love is to accept that one day you must, for a while at least. Guenivere lived to the ripe age of twenty-seven. Eileen kept two small braids from her mane.

In 1991, after the signing of the ADA, outfitters, river runners, and other outdoor adventure companies were required by law to include people with disabilities. Because of her experience at Grand Canyon, Eileen was invited to participate in a pilot project to determine how people with disabilities could be safely accommodated on the Colorado River rafting and camping trips. It was called The River of Dreams and it was a sixteen-day adventure. She was one of eleven people who had disabilities that came from across the country, as well as twenty-one support staff, including outfitters, river guides, and medical personnel.

On this trip, Eileen brought one of Guenivere's braids with her. During a quiet moment near Deer Creek Falls, she placed her braid in the river and watched as it floated away, treasuring her beloved companion and honoring their journey together. The river trip was a great success, and today people with disabilities can raft the Colorado River with their friends and loved ones.

Eileen said goodbye to Zanadu in 1999. They spent nearly twenty years together, gazing up at the stars. She still responded to "Goose-goose", but only for her dearest friends. Her ashes remain in a sacred place, deep within the Camelot soil. Some say they can feel Zanadu's presence behind where Camelot's beautiful, wheelchair accessible (and horse accessible) Labyrinth lays. She was, after all, the goose who found her name written in the stars.

From the very beginning, Eileen knew that, like Josef, she would have to be on the lookout for her own protégé.

"You'll know when that person comes along," said Josef.

In 2002, the person she'd been looking for finally arrived, just as she knew they would. Mary Hadsall embodied all the qualities Eileen considered essential to take Camelot into the future.

After much preparation and planning, Eileen passed the torch to her faithful subjects in 2004. She wanted to give the program the strength to endure without her, and the wings to fly boldly into the future. Many small nonprofit organizations don't survive when the founder leaves, and Eileen would do everything in her power to prevent that from happening.

There was much horse magic to be had between the beginning of Camelot and the passing of the torch, and it continues as Camelot carries on its noble mission. Countless lives have been changed. The lines between student, volunteer, family, friends, and supporters blurred. Eileen built a giant Round Table where everyone could sit and learn from each other, not despite their differences, but because of them.

Lessons that facilitate independence, encourage risk, and set people dreaming couldn't be contained, it was felt by all. And of course, there were horses. Beautiful, magnificent horses at the center of it all.

Josef, also known as Merlin, remained Eileen's mentor. They conducted weekly phone calls, every Wednesday, precisely at 10:45 a.m. Not 10:30. Not 10:50. They also exchanged letters, and his always arrived with a feather and a story. Eileen said goodbye to Josef in 2016, but his presence is with her always. And his lessons live on through Camelot and Rivers Crest Dragon Slayers. Josef's legacy lives on through Camelot.

A couple of young students and their instructor, all on horseback, along with a few volunteers on foot, weave through Camelot's Sonoran Desert landscape. One of the students left her wheelchair behind and is riding the trail on her four-legged partner for the first time. Hooves crunch through the damp sand and the air is thick with the clean scent of creosote. They pass ancient saguaro cacti with arms that reach toward the sky, all topped with blooms.

"What a find!" says a volunteer pointing to a fallen cactus with spines exposed. "It's a saguaro boot."

"What's that?" asks the newer student.

"It's a part of the cactus that was carved out by a bird, maybe a cactus wren. The saguaro forms a hard shell around the exposed flesh to protect itself. It becomes so strong it often outlasts the cactus itself."

"Neat!"

"The pin cushions are topped with a pink crown of flowers right now," says a volunteer to the other student who's blind. "They're a tiny little cactus, about the length of your hand."

The group exits the trail and makes their way around the large, covered arena and past the back of the barn. The horses' hooves clip-clop on the hard-packed dirt driveway that passes the large paddocks where the therapy horses enjoy well-deserved down time.

The instructor stops her horse, "To the right, one of our students, who's also a volunteer, is working in the raised-bed Enchanted Garden. Looks like we'll have tomatoes this year."

"Can I volunteer sometime?" asks the newer student.

"Sure! You can start today by helping me feed dinner."

"Great!"

"We're nearly to the barn. Should we go around again, girls?" the instructor asks.

"Yes!" they both nearly shout at the same time and burst into a fit of giggles.

They pass the barn and take the path that goes between the round pen and the outdoor dressage arena.

"This time around, you girls need to find three natural wonders all on your own. They can be something you see, feel, hear, or smell," says the instructor.

"Smell?" The newer student crinkles her nose.

"It's all fair game!" says the other student with a chuckle.

"Have you girls heard the story about Eileen?" asks the instructor.

"I haven't," says the newer student.

"Well, then you are in for a treat. Some of us call her the Queen of Camelot, but she doesn't like that title," the instructor says with a big grin.

The story of Camelot continues . . .

Some believe Merlin lived time backwards. If indeed this is correct, perhaps the dream of Camelot, the Knights of the Round Table, and the gallant horses that made it all possible began with a young girl of ordinary means named Eileen.

GLOSSARY OF TERMS

Accessible
Easily able to be used, reached, approached, or entered.

Accommodation
1. An adaption or adjustment made
2. Readiness to aid others
3. Lodging

Aristocrat
Someone of nobility or a ruling class or a person having manners and characteristics of nobility.

Americans With Disabilities Act (ADA)
The ADA is an "equal opportunity" law for people with disabilities that was signed into law in 1990. One of the USA's most comprehensive piece of civil rights legislation that prohibits discrimination and guarantees that people with disabilities have the same opportunities as everyone else, including employment. Modeled after the Civil Rights Act of 1964, which prohibits discrimination on the basis of race, color, religion, sex, or national origin and Section 504 of the Rehabilitation Act of 1973. ADA.gov

Adaptive equipment
A tool, device, or machine used to help someone overcome a physical, visual, or auditory impairment with tasks associated with daily living.

Advocate
A person who speaks or writes in defense of another person or cause.

Ally
A person, group, or nation that is associated with another or others for some common cause or purpose.

Architectural barrier
Physical features that limit or prevent people with disabilities from obtaining the goods or services that are offered. They can include parking spaces that are too narrow to accommodate people who use wheelchairs; steps at the entrance of a store; round doorknobs that are difficult to grasp; aisles that are too narrow for a person using a wheelchair, electric scooter, or walker; a high counter or narrow checkout aisles at a cash register; and fixed tables in eating areas that are too low to accommodate a person using a wheelchair or that have fixed seats that prevent a person using a wheelchair from pulling under the table. ADA.gov

Attitude barrier
A way of thinking about a person or a group of people that is negative and limiting. Lack of awareness and stereotypes create a misunderstanding and false assumption about what a person can do,

want, or need. With regards to disability, it's when a non-disabled person doesn't understand how disabilities affect a person's life.

Civil rights
The personal rights guaranteed and protected by the U.S. Constitution and federal laws, such as the Civil Rights Act of 1964 and the ADA of 1990. Civil rights include protection from discrimination. hhs.gov

Deaf or Hard-of-hearing
Having hearing loss ranging from mid to profound.

Dexterity
Skill in performing a physical activity. The ease in using hands for tasks.

Discrimination
Judging a person based on the group, class, or category that person belongs to rather than the individual's merit.

Equality
Being equal.

Inclusion, inclusive
The practice or policy of including all people in activities, organizations, and political processes, such as people living with disabilities.

Intellectually disability
A disability that begins early in the developmental period and involves problems with general mental abilities that affect learning, problem solving and judgment, and/or daily activities such as communication and independent living. Psychiatry.org

Legal Blindness
A definition used by the US government to determine eligibility for vocational training, rehabilitation, schooling, disability benefits, low vision devices and other programs. It doesn't tell us much about what a person can and cannot see. afb.org

Low Vision
Uncorrectable vision loss that interferes with daily activities. afb.org

Misconception
A false idea about someone or something.

Mobility
The state of being mobile or movable, often referring to how a person gets around. For example, some people use wheelchairs or crutches for mobility.

Nonprofit Organization
A business in the United States that doesn't make a profit from its activities. The money raised goes back into their services. A

nonprofit organization has been granted tax-exempt status by the Internal Revenue Service because it provides a public benefit.

People First Language (PFL)

PFL puts the person before the disability and describes what a person has, not who a person is. PFL uses phrases such as "person with a disability," "individuals with disabilities," and "children with disabilities," as opposed to phrases that identify people based solely on their disability, such as "the disabled." DC.gov

Person with a disability

The ADA defines a person with a disability as someone who has a physical or mental impairment that substantially limits one or more major life activities, a person who has a history or record of such impairment, or a person who is perceived by others as having such an impairment. The ADA doesn't specifically name all of the impairments covered. ADA.gov

Physically impaired

A disability that limits a person's capacity to move, coordinate actions, or perform physical activities. It may cause difficulties with motor tasks and independent movement.

Prejudice

Either favorable, unfavorable, or unreasonable opinions and feelings about something or someone without knowledge, thought, or reason. Often, prejudice refers to a hostile nature one may have toward groups of people.

Quadraparetic / Quadraparesis
Partial paralysis or weakness in all four extremities. It differs from quadriplegia because the person has some ability to move and feel their limbs. It could be temporary or permanent and can be brought on by a neuromuscular disease, an infection, or damage to the nervous system.

Quadriplegic / Quadriplegia
Having partial or full paralysis, which is a loss of motor function in the muscles, in both arms and legs.

Stereotype
An oversimplified thought, opinion, or image.

Acknowledgments

Michelle Guerrero

Eileen, thank you for saying yes! I had hoped to write a children's picture book, but instead, you handed me your world. It's not easy putting one's life out for everyone to read; *The Rise of Camelot* is yet another example of your bravery. Telling your story has been my greatest honor, and I will forever treasure the time we spent together bringing this book to fruition. You changed the course of my life when you hired me to work at Camelot in 1999, and I have a feeling you may have done so again. Thanks for giving this horse girl a chance.

My dreams are always big—too big to carry alone. Roy, *mi esposo*, thank you for keeping the family and ranch going while I traveled through time and space, from Santa Cruz to the Grand Canyon—if only in my mind. You are the rock my string is tethered to. *Te amo siempre.*

To my oldest children, Ashley and Jaden, I can always count on you to help me make up my mind and to keep me laughing. Thanks for cheering me on; it's like a double shot of espresso when I need it most! Emilio and Julian, my littles, thanks for letting me write! I know it's oh-so-difficult when robots are invading, and we need to fortify our defenses.

Mom and Dad (aka Jackie and Elliott), your belief in me is powerful magic. Thank you both for being my first editors and fiercest Scrabble competitors. And thanks for hauling me to the barn, the riding lessons, and, of course, the horses. The time and energy you poured into me all these years set me up for this gig.

To my sisters, Laura and Sue, the coolest cats on Guilford Road, I've always looked up to you. Thank you for teaching me to be strong.

Beta readers, I am grateful for you. Mary Westheimer, Stacey Corrigan, Mary Hadsall, Denise Thompson, Susan Marks, and Tracie Collier, your input and attention to detail helped make our manuscript shine. Thanks for letting me lean on you. Mary H., I also appreciate you being our official Camelot archivist. Mary W., thanks for editing my work and perfecting my skills since the turn of the century. I'm thrilled we had another Camelot project to work on together.

Mark Bogosian, when I asked you to write our foreword, I knew two things about you: One, your job with the Christopher & Dana Reeve Foundation gave you the ability to grant wishes to nonprofit organizations dedicated to improving the quality of life for individuals and families impacted by paralysis. Secondly, even though you had this big, important job, you were the kind of person who would reach out with kind words to a grant writer for a small organization. Thank you for writing the foreword for our book! The support from you and the Christopher and Dana Reeve Foundation is an invaluable gift that gives me courage.

Casie Bazay, I remember meeting you around 2016, when we were contenders for a writing mentorship program. Two horse girls, writing for magazines, and working hard for the day we could call ourselves book authors. Eileen and I are fortunate to have a talented editor and published author like you edit *The Rise of Camelot*. Thank you!

Judi Lauren, my friend and mentor, I would be remiss if I didn't include you in every book I ever write. Your advice is always with me. I edit with your lessons in my heart and your choice of coffee in my cup. Thank you for all you've taught me. Sonya Weiss, my southern sister, thank you for your steadfast encouragement. But most importantly, thanks for teaching me that book-writing careers don't all fit in the same size box. I don't know if I would have had the courage to fly had you not taught me that.

Rebecca Acord, thank you for selling my books in your shop, Sweet Country Charm Fudge & Gifts in Payson, Arizona, and for the constant stream of delicious, thought-provoking fudge! Shannon Devra Ropp, thanks for marketing my books locally, keeping me on my toes, and making me laugh. You are a beautiful, bright spot in the world.

Students of Camelot, your spirits lit the spark. Your strength and courage fanned the flame that I would one day write a book that reflected your grit. I'm grateful to sit at Camelot's Round Table with you. Leadership Through Horsemanship teens who are now adults, I can still hear your laughter in the Camelot barn as we made up a silly story about a Gila monster, and you encouraged me to write it for real. Thank you for dreaming with me, and one day, that book might still happen.

Writing acknowledgements is indeed one of the most important and difficult things to do. If I have neglected to include you, please accept my apology. Many people have helped me bring this book to fruition, and I'm fortunate to have you in my life.

Book lovers, thanks for reading. May you, too, dream big and embark on your own quest. Be brave, because they're rarely easy. Be strong, for you'll be tested. And remember, wherever you're going, the place you're seeking is seeking you!

Eileen Szychowski

It was September of 2020 when my former colleague Michelle Guerrero reached out to me about an idea for a children's book. The world was in lockdown from the Covid 19 pandemic, everyone wondering how this worldwide event was going to play out. I hadn't chatted with Michelle in quite some time but kept up to date on her life through mutual friends. I knew that she had moved to the rim country of Payson, Arizona, where she and her family were enjoying the simple pleasures of small town living and ranch life. I also knew that she was making a living as a freelance writer and author of children's books, something that had been a lifelong dream for her. Michelle already had a number of books for children and young readers in the fiction genre, but now she wanted to try her hand at nonfiction for children, specifically, a biography.

Over the years, I'd been approached more than once to do something with my life story and my work with horses and people with disabilities. My answer had always been no, largely because most journalists and screenwriters are incapable of writing about disability issues without resorting to sensational, overly dramatic language that causes problems for those of us living with disabilities. Another reason for turning down such offers is that I have never been in favor of people making money off of me or anyone else in the disability community — too many of us are still struggling to find adequate employment, housing, and healthcare.

But Michelle's proposal was different than all the others. For starters, she proposed producing this book as a fundraising tool for Camelot Therapeutic Horsemanship, Inc., a nonprofit program I started many years ago. In other words, neither she, nor I, nor any other person would receive any compensation whatsoever; the book would be intended as an ongoing revenue stream for Camelot, a program that offers its services for free. I also knew from experience that Michelle Guerrero is a talented writer who is capable of writing about disability issues in a straightforward, dignified way. In other words, she was the right person asking at the right time and in the right way. So, perhaps to her surprise and my own, I said yes, confident that she would do justice to the story and the cause. And she has done precisely that (I love it when I can say "I told you so" to myself!). I'm proud of the book she has created and more grateful to her that I can express, for without Michelle Guerrero, this book would not have come to pass.

There are many other individuals who also helped make this book a reality, but before I go any further, I wish to extend my lifelong gratitude and deepest respect to the people in the disability community on whose shoulders I stand: people like Ed Roberts, Justin Dart, and Judy Heumann, to name a few. Their names may not be recognizable outside the disability community, but they are giants nonetheless, and the entire disability community and its allies owe them a debt of gratitude for the rights we enjoy today.

I also wish to thank Jan Cutler of the Fred Harvey Company; Karen Berggren, JT Reynolds, Superintendent Richard Marks and Scott Berkenfield of the National Park Service for the doors they opened to me. Without their advocacy and support, there would not have been a disabled ranger on horseback at Grand Canyon National Park.

There are many others I wish to acknowledge as well: Vicki Bloom, who generously opened her home to a stranger with a goose; Rita Gannon of Santa Rita Stables for hosting us before we had a home of our own; and the Curriculum Development Committee: Pam Ludwig, Gail Curran, Lauren DeVuyst, Denise Thompson, and Shirley Lowman, whose dedication and hard work during Camelot's infancy led to the development of a vibrant educational curriculum still in use today.

And where would Camelot be without the contribution of veterinarians Dr. Mike McDole and Dr. Vicki Baumler who, from the very beginning, donated their services, keeping Camelot's horses healthy and happy in their jobs. More than thirty-five years later, Dr. Baumler continues to serve as Camelot's primary veterinarian.

My thanks also to Tracie Collier, Mary Hadsall, Susan Marks, Denise Thompson, and Mary Westheimer, who from the outset have provided invaluable support and advice on the book.

I am also grateful to Mark Bogosian of the Christopher and Dana Reeve Foundation for his enthusiastic support of the book and the work being done at Camelot.

I will also be forever grateful to the countless donors and sponsors whose generosity turned the dream of Camelot into a reality and continue to keep the flame alive forty years later. They, along with our dedicated volunteers, are the life-giving element so critical to the day-to-day operations of therapeutic riding programs everywhere. Thank you for making the magic happen!

For all of the students who come to Camelot – past, present, and future – I salute you! Keep slaying those dragons!

Last but not least, my eternal gratitude to Josef Rivers, a teacher without equal and an English gentleman in every sense of the word. Without him there would be no Camelot, and I would still be swimming in a very small pond instead of the ocean of possibilities that have blessed my life.

As for you, dear reader, by purchasing this book you are helping to further the work of Camelot, for which I thank you. May each of you be fortunate enough to have your life intersect with an individual who reveals to you your unique gifts and responsibilities and may you one day pay it forward by being that individual for someone else.

The Author

The ink was barely dry on Michelle Guerrero's diploma from Arizona State University's Walter Cronkite School of Journalism when she decided it would be more exciting to work outdoors with horses and people than in an office.

In 1999, Michelle interviewed with Eileen Szychowski, the executive director of Camelot Therapeutic Horsemanship, Inc., and was hired as a barn manager and riding instructor. This was her dream job—one that would utilize her education, life-long passion for horses, and experience working with people who had disabilities.

Eileen's commanding presence and quick wit were magnetic. She taught Michelle to make wings because sometimes being an advocate and an ally is less about handholding and more about teaching someone to fly. Before long, she saw Eileen as a mentor and friend. They shared a love of horses, the outdoors, Arthurian legend, and Italian food.

Through the years, Michelle had several roles at Camelot, including volunteer coordinator, director of community relations, and grant writer. She moved on in 2013 to be a stay-at-home mom, but to be honest, she never really left. While she doesn't work at the ranch, she still has a few titles: volunteer editor, supporter, and friend.

She's a mom of four who lives in a cabin in the woods with her husband and two youngest boys. She's often spotted walking through the trees, surrounded by horses, pups, goats, and kids. She grew up in Illinois but moved to Arizona when perms were still a thing.

Michelle is the author of a young adult series (*Winged: a Unicorn Queen Novel*), and three children's books (*The Christmas Witch, Mud Pies: A Story About Moving Through Grief and Finding Happiness,* and *The Runaway Wish*). **MichelleGuerrero.com**

Michelle is signing with Sara, a student and friend who's Deaf.

Michelle with students during Camelot's Hooves & Heroes open house in 2011. Photo by Kristyn Moore.

Michelle teaching Keri, a visually impaired student, how to pick hooves in 2003.

Camelot
Scrapbook

LIFE IN THE REDWOODS

Eileen and Zanadu, visiting
Mark Mathews' class.

Josef Rivers circa 1988.

Eileen riding Scarlett.
Photo by CH 11 News.

Eileen cantering sidesaddle on
Scarlett. Photo by CH 11 News.

Photo by Karen Berggren

Zanadu, Eileen and FBC kids, circa 1988.

THE GRAND CANYON

Eileen and Guenivere.
Photo by Connie Rudd,
courtesy of The
National Park Service.

Photos by Connie Rudd, courtesy of the National Park Service.

Eileen teaching on the rim.

A National Park Service patch found in Eileen's mementos. These patches appeared on the sleeve of all her uniforms.

Eileen riding the mules in the canyon.
Photo by Bob Rink, AZ Highways,
March 1997.

Photo by Mike Valentine,
a park visitor.

Eileen and Tina
Hutton in 1982.
Park visitor turned
life-long friend.

THE QUEENDOM

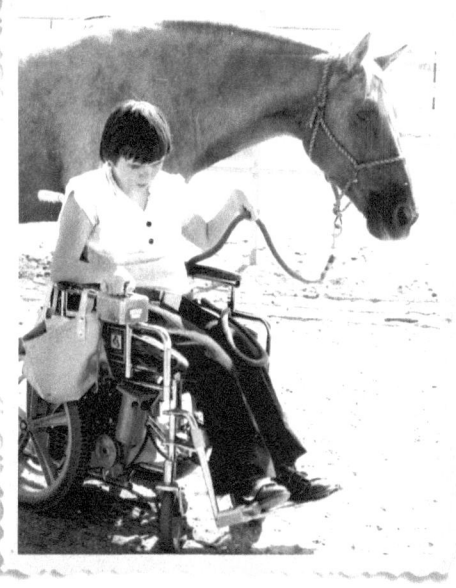

A Camelot student learns to lead Guenivere. Photo by Karen Berggren, 1983.

Photo by Barb Bailey, Camelot volunteer.

Denise Thompson, a rider with a visual impairment and one of Camelot's first students, learns about hoof picks from Lauren. Photo by Karen Berggren, 1983.

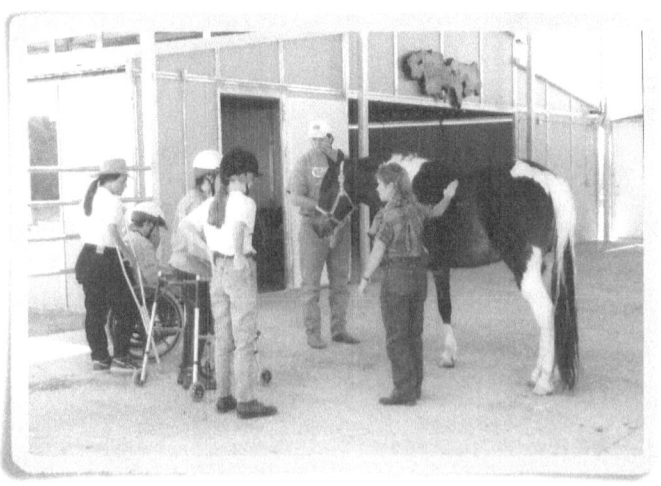

Mike Covert, Camelot's first barn manager, holds Scout during a lesson.

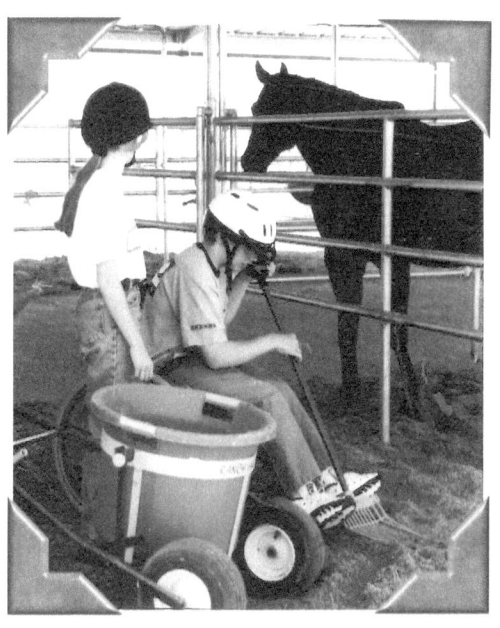

Camelot students cleaning
stalls together.

Joe Hogg, a Camelot friend,
visits with Glory, an Arabian
horse. Glory touches her nose
to the word "welcome" on Joe's
communication board.
Photo by Barb Bailey.

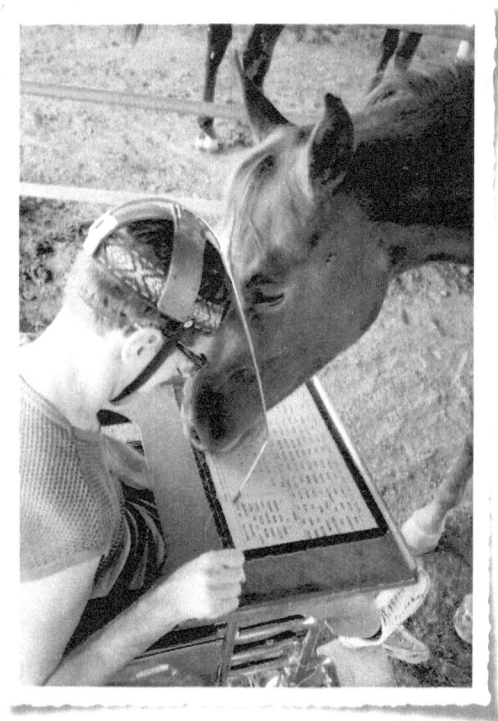

THE CAMELOT CREED

Written in 1986 by Eileen Szychowski

We believe dreams are essential to life and the right to risk belongs to us all,
We commit ourselves to slaying the dragons of doubt in ourselves and others,
We believe the world is changed one life at a time,
We dedicate ourselves to a program designed for the individual, wherein quality will always be placed before quantity,
We believe persons with disabilities should be in control of their own lives,
We pledge ourselves to a program where disabled people govern themselves and a learning model based on mentorship,
We believe freedom and dignity are priceless; success can only be kept when given away,
We commit ourselves to a Camelot which will always be free of charge other than the commitment to become a contributor to our community,
We believe life is a Round Table wherein each member is both student and teacher,
We pledge to build in each other the knightly virtues of Courage, Loyalty, Compassion, Honor, Justice, Generosity, and Faith,
We believe in the philosophy of Camelot, which calls on each of us to rise to our highest good,
We embrace the Quest and dedicate ourselves to quality life with programs that offer opportunities to dream, to risk, to love, and to serve.

Eileen speaking at Camelot's Grand
Opening, February 1998.

"The unsinkable" Lynn Martinka,
a student and polio survivor, at
Camelot's blessing ceremony.

Riders enjoy greater access to nature on horseback. Photo by Hamilton Wright, Jr.

March 1998

River's Crest Dragon Slayers
Therapeutic Horsemanship for the Handicapped
A Non-Profit Organization

Josef Rivers
Director

My Dearly Beloved Queen of Camelot,

I was so touched for you to mention me in your cover letter at your grand opening. It is a very comforting feeling to know now that Camelot is complete and is under your complete control, as well it should be. It is important you have your beloved horses gather about you that you might fall asleep listening to them munching their hay and it is so vitally important to me that you own your own facility and that you are safe and happy with it. You have created such a comfortable place for my spirit to dwell. You are my citadel and your success is my contentment. Look about, I am with you, Camelot is my home also.

Your devoted teacher,
Merlin

On horseback, disabilities are left behind. Photo by Barb Bailey.

Eileen teaching a
student to drive Sandy,
a miniature horse.

Camelot's 20th
anniversary.
Photo by Dan Webber.

The future home of Camelot. Photo by Hamilton Wright, Jr.

CAMELOT THEN AND NOW...

Aerial view of Camelot. Drone photo courtesy of Ray Klein.

The sword in the stone, 2023.

Whosoever shall pulleth
this Sword from this Stone
shall be rightwise born a Hero

The Camelot barn in 2018.

Cliffy, a therapy horse, walking
the labyrinth in 2011. Photos by
Mary Hadsall.

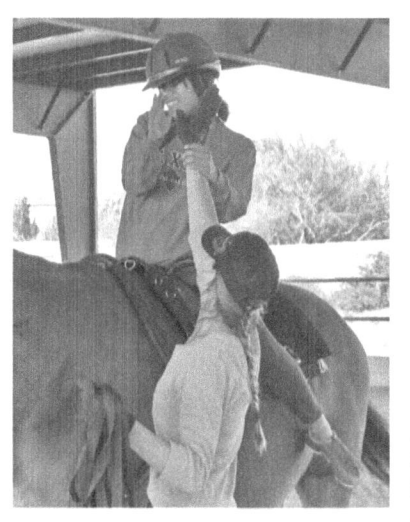

Mary Hadsall giving a high-
five to Andrea, a visually
impaired student, 2010.

Mary Hadsall, Eileen's successor as
Camelot's executive director, 2004.

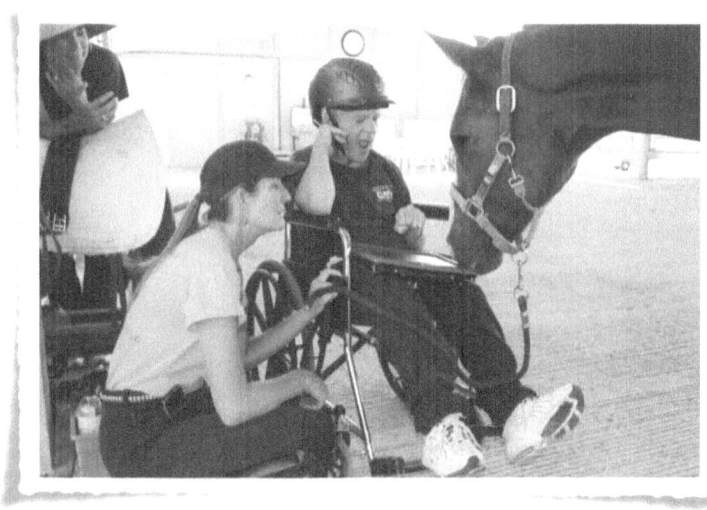

Hayden, a student, using his communication devise while
Cliffy joins the conversation, 2010.

In order: Michelle, Jessica, Hayden, and Mary.
Riding demonstration for Hooves & Heroes 2008.

Where Heroes Are Born

"In short there's simply not a more congenial spot for happily everafter-ing than here in Camelot." Lyrics by Alan Jay Lerner from the musical "Camelot"

"Take up your sword against the most formidable enemy of all, the voice within that says, 'I can't.'" ~ Eileen Szychowski

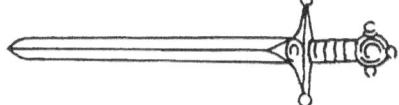

CamelotAZ.org

www.ingramcontent.com/pod-product-compliance
Lightning Source LLC
Chambersburg PA
CBHW020245130626
46549CB00005B/2063